Leg Avant

The New Poetry of Cricket

Leg Avant

The New Poetry of Cricket

EDITED BY R.T.A. PARKER

ISBN
978-1-326-46922-1

ISSN
2041-0948

CRATER 35

Izmir–London

February 2016

CONTENTS

RICHARD PARKER

The New Poetry of Cricket

Of all games, cricket embodies life's passions most richly. It can, too, be unspeakably boring, as drab and futile as a pointless journey.

MICHAEL BREARLEY

You're a fool if you think your system will give you cricket much longer.

MICHAEL ROBERTS

My original intention for this book was to gather poems that brought together both a capacious experimental clarity and the high, clear seriousness of cricket. On reflection the project would seem to have been somewhat quixotic. Firstly, I hadn't yet read or written or imagined a poem that could have met such a demand (C.L.R. James's *Beyond a Boundary* must be the greatest poem of cricket—but it's not a poem). Secondly, cricket is not all that high or serious. I decided, then, that I would seek a cricketing poetry that might at least avoid nostalgia.

But cricket *is* nostalgia, of course. Pernicious, imperial nostalgia. It is the English national game, the game of empire; class and race are embedded in its organisational structure; it was a significant element of the self-identity of viciously segregated societies in Africa, Australia, the Caribbean and the Indian subcontinent—a tool against and for struggles for independence and civil wars. All of this is contained in the marmalade stripes of cricketing nostalgia. We might assume that the poetry of cricket must, then, be a reactionary poetry, and for the most part it is. Thus William Wordsworth, in 1802, associated cricket with a counter-revolutionary England, standing firm against the dislocations of post-revolutionary France. 'Composed in the valley near Dover, on the day of landing':

> Here, on our native soil, we breathe once more.
> The cock that crows, the smoke that curls, that sound
> Of bells; those boys who in yon meadow-ground
> In white-sleeved shirts are playing; and the roar
> Of the waves breaking on the chalky shore;—
> All, all are English. Oft have I looked round
> With joy in Kent's green vales; but never found
> Myself so satisfied in heart before.
> Europe is yet in bonds; but let that pass,
> Thought for another moment. Thou art free,
> My Country! and 'tis joy enough and pride
> For one hour's perfect bliss, to tread the grass
> Of England once again, and hear and see,
> With such a dear Companion at my side.

Tony Collins identifies Wordsworth's connection of cricket and English society as 'a variation of the "Merrie England" myth in which feudal England was viewed as bucolic idyll of deferential social harmony'; 'a yearning for the neverland of the rural past'. Wordsworth's anxiousness to leave France (the Terror, his own sexual incontinence) is assuaged by the soporific inaction of village cricket, and the comfort blanket of a Tory, reactionary England. This is the kind of thinking about cricket that gets Nigel Farage down to the St Lawrence Ground.

Ninety years later, the sentimental slough of late-Victoriana, this is Henry Newbolt's even balder call to cricketing arms, 'Vitaï Lampada', the most famous and malign cricket poem of them all:

> There's a breathless hush in the Close to-night—
> Ten to make and the match to win—
> A bumping pitch and a blinding light,
> An hour to play and the last man in.
> And it's not for the sake of a ribboned coat,
> Or the selfish hope of a season's fame,
> But his captain's hand on his shoulder smote
> 'Play up! play up! and play the game!'
>
> The sand of the desert is sodden red,—
> Red with the wreck of a square that broke;—
> The Gatling's jammed and the Colonel dead,
> And the regiment blind with dust and smoke.
> The river of death has brimmed his banks,
> And England's far, and Honour a name,
> But the voice of a schoolboy rallies the ranks:
> 'Play up! play up! and play the game!'
>
> This is the word that year by year,
> While in her place the school is set,
> Every one of her sons must hear,
> And none that hears it dare forget.
> This they all with a joyful mind
> Bear through life like a torch in flame,

And falling fling to the host behind—
'Play up! play up! and play the game!'

Newbolt's poem is a call to the sacrifice of British blood upon the altar of empire, but it also contains the seeds of an imperial superiority—of a celebration of the blood of British boys and the discarding of the blood of inferior foreigners; of the celebration of the public school officer and the careless destruction of the man of the ranks. As Derek Birley writes, the poem's 'sentiments [...] were those that sustained the flower of British youth as they bore the White Man's Burden into the remote corners of empire.' Exhortations to empire and an imperial nostalgia will be key areas to avoid for this anthology—but we will not be able to rid ourselves of nostalgia completely. Perhaps we might imagine the quite different tone of A.E. Housman's nostalgic cricket poetry as a corrective to Newbolt's blood-thirstiness. Another key late-Victorian text, Housman's *A Shropshire Lad*, once again features sport as analogue for war, though in a different mode from Newbolt. This is poem XVII:

Twice a week the winter thorough
Here stood I to keep the goal:
Football then was fighting sorrow
For the young man's soul.

Now in Maytime to the wicket
Out I march with bat and pad:
See the son of grief at cricket
Trying to be glad.

Try I will; no harm in trying:
Wonder 'tis how little mirth
Keeps the bones of man from lying
On the bed of earth.

There are different kinds of nostalgia; Newbolt's is a Virgilian, martial nostalgia; the Tory/Augustan's anxious return to a golden age of social order and the recreation of that order in empire, just as Wordsworth's fright at France urges him towards the use of cricket as a prop for nationalism—his cricketing Ithacans exemplars of a Wellingtonian might as much as an English pastoralism. Housman, though he uses a similar conceit to Newbolt and sings a Wordsworthian rusticity, offers a divergent nostalgia. Where Newbolt propagandistically sweetens warfare by comparing it to schoolboy sport, Housman's 'son of grief at cricket' reveals the deadly masque of the public school playing field, a complete reversal of the imperial procedure. Where Newbolt's nostalgia, then, is Virgilian, pushing his lads outward towards empire, we can think of Housman's as Homeric, drawn back from and refusing war, honour and wrath in order to return to the variegated greens of that public school cricketing nostos. The deathly and plangent nostalgia of Francis Thompson's 'At Lords' inhabits a similar place.

Carol Watts's 'Crease', with which this volume begins, is perhaps the most Housman-esque of the poems here—it addresses Watts's father, the Northamptonshire left-handed middle order batsman and captain Jim Watts, and life in a working-class cricketing family far from Newbolt's playing fields—but Housman's cricketing nostalgia is featured throughout *Leg*

Avant. Alan Halsey's, Jeff Hilson's, Ben Hickman's, Peter Hughes's and John Hall's pieces all certainly tend towards this kind of nostalgic—not Newboltian—cricket. Chris Hall's 'why i do not play cricket' offers an interesting derangement of cricketing nostalgia, retaining the retrospective tone and familiar playing-fields setting from the cricket-memoir, but recasting it as traumatic primal scene.

In *BLAST*, Wyndham Lewis 'blasts' (gentleman) C.B. Fry and 'blesses' (player) George Hirst alongside Newbolt, a move which seems an ironic assertion of the dialectical capacity of cricket; its ability to simultaneously assert the revolutionary and the counter-revolutionary. Cricket is nostalgia but it is also revolution. Cricket has been a crucial channel for resistance and redress in the national struggles of almost every cricketing nation. Political backgrounds cast very different lights on passages of cricket. We can compare the brutal dourness of English Bodyline in the 1930s with the joyously physical West Indian and Australian fast bowling of the 1970s. Both England and her dominions transgressed the conventional mores of cricket in these moments, but where Douglas Jardine's strategy was brutal and Newboltian in support of the claims and assumptions of empire, Andy Roberts, Michael Holding, Joel Garner and Colin Croft's—or Jeff Thomson and Dennis Lillee's—ferocity was gleeful and liberatory when directed towards the imperial centre.

The new poems of cricket will not resemble 'Vitaï Lampada' and their sport will be the cricket of resistance and imperial redress. It will also approach the revolutionary language of the avant-garde. Ludwig Wittgenstein is supposed to have liked cricket, perhaps even its distinctive terminology, and there is something in the peculiarity of the cricketing vocabulary and the declensions of the scorecard that brings to mind the self-consciously alienating language of experimental literature. Samuel Beckett is in *Wisden*—the most famous cricketing avantist—but he never wrote about cricket directly, though the slow drabness of the sport may have found its way into Beckett's texts. James Joyce played, 'promised to be a useful bat' according to his brother John Stanislaus, and approached the game briefly but interestingly in his writing. This passage shows how he made use of the language of cricket in *Finnegans Wake*:

> Kickakick. She had to kick a laugh. At her old stick-in-the-block. The way he was slogging his paunch about, elbiduubled, meet oft mate on, like hale King Willow, the robberer. Cainmaker's mace and waxened capapee. But the tarrant's brand on his hottoweyt brow. At half past quick in the morning. And her lamp was all askew and a trumbly wick-in-her, ringeysingey. She had to spofforth, she had to kicker, too thick of the wick of her pixy's loomph, wide lickering jessup the smooky shiminey. And her duffed coverpoint of a wickedy batter, whenever she druv behind her stumps for a tyddlesly wink through his tunnilcleff bagslops after the rising bounder's yorkers, as he studd and stoddard and trutted and trumpered, to see had lordherry's blackham's red bobby abbels, it tickled her innings to consort pitch at kicksolock in the morm. Tipatonguing him on in her pigeony linguish, with a flick at the bails

> for lubrication, to scorch her faster, faster. Ye hek, ye hok, ye hucky hiremonger! Magrath he's my pegger, he is, for bricking up all my old kent road. He'll win your toss, flog your old tom's bowling and I darr ye, barrackybuller, to break his duck! He's posh. I lob him. We're parring all Oogster till the empsyseas run googlie. Declare to ashes and teste his metch! Three for two will do for me and he for thee and she for you. Goeasyosey, for the grace of the fields, or hooley pooley, cuppy, we'll both be bye and by caught in the slips for fear he'd tyre and burst his dunlops and waken her bornybarnies making his boobybabies. The game old merri-mynn, square to leg, with his lolleywide towelhat and his hobbsy socks and his wisden's bosse and his norsery pinafore and his gentleman's grip and his playaboy's plunge and his flannelly feelyfooling, treading her hump and hambledown like a maiden wellheld, ovalled over, with her crease where the pads of her punishments ought to be by womanish rights when, keek, the hen in the doran's shantyqueer began in a kikkery key to laugh it off, yeigh, yeigh, neigh, neigh, the way she was wuck to doodle-doo by her gallows bird (how's that? Noball, he carries his bat!) nine hundred and dirty too not out, at all times long past conquering cock of the morgans.

Joyce includes a series of players here (at least 43 have been identified—among them K.S. Ranjitsinhji, F.R. Spofforth, G.L. Jessop, A.E. Trott, Victor Trumper, George Parr, W.G. Grace, 'Gubby' Allen, Sir Jack Hobbs), who are listed in a kind of hallucination of the empirical code of the score sheet. Alongside them Joyce also includes a welter of deranged cricketing terms and positions ('elbiduubled' etc.), picking up on and elaborating the innate strangeness of cricketing vocabulary as he does with so many other argots in the *Wake*. This kind of cricketing echolalia can be found throughout this volume. Jèssica Pujol Duran's Catalan and Tim Atkins and Chiaki Matsubayashi's bilingual English/Japanese pieces relate some of the fascination that the magic of the words of cricket hold for the non-Anglophone. The Canadian Peter Jaeger's 'Summer Haiku (after Leonard Cohen)' similarly foregrounds the strangeness of this game in the eyes of the world, while Geraldine Monk, Ken Edwards, Scott Thurston and Antony John all exploit cricket's lexicon, each pursuing distinctive kennings, mishearings and new constructions that re-contextualise the wordbook of cricket in an avant-garde context. This is the same radical unfamiliarity that energises Gregorio Fontaine and Montenegro Fisher's contributions; an unfamiliarity marked at its close with the connection of the profound strangeness of cricket with the British imperial project—a parallel that also shows us the avant-garde as the stormtroopers of the liberal-bourgeois revolution. Rhys Trimble uses cricket as a, rather dubious, cultural artefact in a way that can be compared with Joyce's method, though he excitingly refuses glossolalia. Andrew Spragg, on the other hand, develops the revolutionary potential of this kind of language a step further by providing an explicit connection between the language of capital and the euphemistic language of order that cricket developed on the playing fields of Dulwich College.

Almost everything can be found in *Finnegans Wake*, however. Joyce's inclusivity is predicated on the idea that anything might be manhandled into literature, and the less literary the better. Cricket can sneak into the avant-garde here, effectively through the back door, precisely because of its irrelevance. It gets into the *Wake* because its lists are material, strange and, most importantly, futile—that the author played in childhood is really neither here nor there, and there is little sense that Joyce is offering any profound critique of the sport. Cricket enters the avant-garde at numerous points due to this dubious rationale. Peter Riley, introducing a selection of poems by Nicholas Moore for Iain Sinclair's anthology *Conductors of Chaos*, exemplifies this tendency:

> Since nobody was listening, the poetry could be 'anything'. Long meditations, short epigrams, rhymed and unrhymed, measured and unmeasured, sonnets, songs, ballads, blues, straight philosophical statements, symbolic landscapes, surrealist figurations, imagist trances, jokes and nonsense, poems in gobbledegook, outrageous travesty and satire, calm description, detective poems, jazz poems, cricket poems, haiku, doggerel, pure 1940s lyrics and *persona* narratives... all 'rubbish', all free as the wind.

Riley does not include any of Moore's 'cricket poems' in *Conductors of Chaos*, and cricket, here, is precisely the non-poetic; the 'rubbish' not fit for poetry. Here the sport has lost some of its imperial colouring and perhaps assumed its other stereotype; that of overcast afternoons, rain delays and the numerate bores of the pavilion.

This is the same tone that we find in the greatest of cricketing films, Alfred Hitchcock's *The Lady Vanishes* (1938)—a cricket film in spite of the fact that its cricket is endlessly delayed and finally elided. In the characters of Charters and Caldicott, the boorish, closeted Englishman sublimates desire and his wilful ignorance of the spectral oppressions at play around him into a destructive, all-consuming, deadening obsession with the game. Charters and Caldicott never get there, of course, the Old Trafford Test to which they so blindly, amorally, rush towards is a wash out. Their inaction throughout the film, barring a late flurry of bravery at the conclusion, reproduces the carelessness of England before its empire and the myopia of the middle-classes in the midst of it.

Tony Lopez's contribution to this volume, the last section of his long poem *Radial Symmetry*, represents a certain strand of the avant-garde's critique of this understanding of the insipid world of cricket. Lopez's 'uncle running up to bowl, Someone / sampling smut. Taste of lemons and oysters' encapsulates middle-class English male life; its onanism, the market and the *bon vivants* in the corporate suites are inseparably aligned with the musty English blandness of the mid-century; the innuendo that lies beneath it all.

Manifestations of baseball in American avant-grade poetry offer a possible model for the new poetry of cricket. Baseball appears more frequently there than cricket tends to in the experimental poetries of Britain, and with a cultural valence and lack of anxiety that are quite different from most British avant-grade representations of cricket. Baseball has a notable position in the American experimental tradition, featuring at significant—if rarely central—points in the works of poets from

Walt Whitman through William Carlos Williams and Marianne Moore, the Objectivists, the New American Poetry and up to the Language Poets and beyond. For some writers, including Jack Spicer, Kenneth Koch, Ted Berrigan and Ron Silliman, baseball appears almost compulsively in their work, providing a refrain; a cultural detailing or a grain of American experience from outside of the academy and poetry that proves key in the cultural positioning of these poets. There is a similarity in their representation of baseball, however, with the National Pastime standing, pretty inertly, as a social referent—a symbol of the American Working Man (very unlike Charters and Caldicott), American childhood, the American past and the American unpoetic. Williams's 'The Crowd at the Ball Game' is a useful example of the default poetic attitude towards baseball. His poem begins:

> The crowd at the ball game
> is moved uniformly
>
> by a spirit of uselessness
> which delights them—
>
> all the exciting detail
> of the chase
>
> and the escape, the error
> the flash of genius—
>
> all to no end save beauty
> the eternal—

Williams makes the democratic gesture of concerning himself with the unpoetic subjects of baseball and its mass consumption, but his discomfort with the crowd and his disconnection from their sport is palpable. We see nothing of the grace of the hitter swinging, nor the beautiful parabola of the rising fly ball and the flash of tension before it drops—nor yet the revolutionary potential of such moments—those instants are, instead, dismissed as 'the exciting detail', a concern of the amorphous crowd but not of the poet.

For some writers, however, baseball, while retaining its particular cultural significance, offers a more important understanding of the world. This is particularly the case for Spicer. In his verse it becomes far more than a sport; the location of utopian possibility and the potential manifestation of a *Paradiso terrestre* on the North American West Coast. After watching minor-league baseball in Vancouver with George Bowering, Spicer wrote the following poem, the first of his 'Seven Poems for the Vancouver Festival':

> Start with a baseball diamond high In the Runcible
>   Mountain wilderness. Blocked everywhere by
> stubborn lumber. Where even the ocean cannot reach its
> coastline for the lumber of islands or the river of its
>   mouth. A perfect diamond with a right field, center
>   field, left field of
> felled logs spreading vaguely outward. Four sides each
>   Facet of the diamond.
> We shall build our city backwards from each
>   baseline extending like a square ray from each
>   distance—you from the first-base line, you from

behind the second baseman, you from behind the
short stop, you from the third-baseline.
We shall clear the trees back, the lumber of our pasts
and futures back, because we are on a diamond,
because it is our diamond
Pushed forward from.
And our city shall stand as the lumber rots and Runcible
mountain crumbles, and the ocean, eating all of
islands, comes to meet us.

Spicer imagines the splayed foul lines of the baseball diamond spreading eastwards, infinitely, carving up the American continent and providing a utopian city plan with their endlessness. It is the nature of the baseball diamond that it is at once limited and limitless; only two sides of the diamond are open (the others provide the foul lines), but the other two sides—that must be crossed to provide the elusive home run—open onto the infinite and the endlessly possible, with unpainted but foul lines endlessly running alongside them. A more rhizomatic utopianism might emerge from the 360° of the cricket boundary, perhaps, in distinction to the linearity of Spicer's reversal of Lewis and Clark.

But there are some obvious reasons why it hasn't achieved the same poetic ubiquity as baseball, nor elicited the surreally transcendent heights of Spicer. Different understandings of class in both poetry and sport make the American version impossible in England, while the absence of a Whitman from the English national consciousness and an American sense of scale precludes such grand gestures. The effectiveness with which Spicer speaks to empire might seem readily and usefully applicable to a critique-lead poetry of cricket, however, and is comparable with the impetus behind the Australian poet Nick Whittock's contribution to this volume, 'Fiery James Fallkners'. It is perhaps necessary that it is an Australian who provides the grandest and strangest vision of cricket in this volume—the frontier, open spaces; the ferocious enthusiasm of Australian cricket and the continuous newness that it provides the sport, are closer to the expansive Whitmanian vision than the modulated nostalgias of the English game and English poetry about cricket.

Finally, while we have noted cricket's function in combating the legacies of an empire that it was originally tasked with supporting, we should also consider the necessity that an avant-garde poetry of cricket must continue to extend this liberatory possibility; the concerns of an avant-garde cricketing poetry will not be solely with empire, but also with class, the patriarchy and the environment. Americans—perhaps Moore and Koch—might give us models for using the poetries of baseball and cricket as an instrument of class warfare, while Spicer offers us a starting point for an ecological poetry of sport. Spicer doesn't, however, come close to offering a route towards a feminist poetry of cricket. Some poets in this volume do, however. Sarah Kelly's and Nia Davies's poems demonstrate a discomfort with the irredeemably masculinized world of professional sports and the cult of conformist competition that it promotes—their poems pivoting on critiques of cricket as points from which to address deeper difficulties.

Avant Leg has proved a far different volume than the one I first imagined, and I think a better one. But like the Runcible

Mountain diamond, like the boundary rope and like cricket itself, the vast bulk of this anthology is potential and utopian, extending over the horizon and never to be written. The ever-coming revolution in verse; the sound of windows smashing, hoofs and sirens; the crack of the willow.

CAROL WATTS

Crease

What do they know of cricket
who only cricket know
CLR JAMES

behind the popping crease
you won't be called out

not by flamboyant trees   or
night boundaries   scores

'whipped hot from the pitch'
& totalled by magicians

on rainy afternoons turned
interminable   suddenly

to make a continual return
forced to find form   each

season confronted with
youth   the old machinery

standing there in threads
& pavilions   as white as

women made them   waiting
at the gate   each

proud summer   collecting
clippings from correspondents

& radio voices   the world
coming through car parks

to witness philosophies of
uncertainty & prediction

cerebral balancing of left
with right   intimations of climate

variation brought to decision
& long English   shadows

so long I thought death could
be stayed by etiquette

& principle   like summer was
in Bishan Bedi's spin

coaxed beyond the crease   to risk
each instant   everything in flight

JEFF HILSON

From the Almanack

Whenever I think of england
I think in the long grass
of the toughened veins
of david steele
on warm summer days playing
and missing in the dark
for five and a quarter hours.
Oh to dig a tunnel
with a straight bat in the field
of house cricket
house cricket which will not survive
the english winter.
With glandular fever
I hooked old for six
on the short sward
I was almost my normal
temperature
not out
against the opening bowler gurr
when I made that classic stridulatory call

to tavaré:
Dear chris how is it
at the vauxhall end?
In the rain he toiled in the long nineteen
seventies
when there were eleven men
in the world
with a new ball.
In spring the right arm queens emerge
moving in the air of the minor counties
staying there and staying there and
underarm.
Even I wanted to strengthen my side.
But the oval is only
a southern cricket ground
slow and dusty
and without a sainsburys
at the pavilion end.
Back in england the radio changed everything.
By the gasometers women lift the ball
their beautiful actions
which have never been recorded
produce a noise
DO NOT CLICK ON THEM
carrying across the A202
perhaps they carry on around the wicket
where david steele is not a good analogy
his modified legs
sinking in the damp substrate
and genital organs
banging it in.

Old I obviously french cut Tavaré
is my shepherd I'll
not walk
again in this golden age of adult
cricket he replied
tossing on the field of play
with his enormous gillette head
and TMS.
It must be all square at the surrey station.
Mushtaq mohammed is coming
in grass hopper gloves.
I am setting my field for autumn.
England is flamboyant.

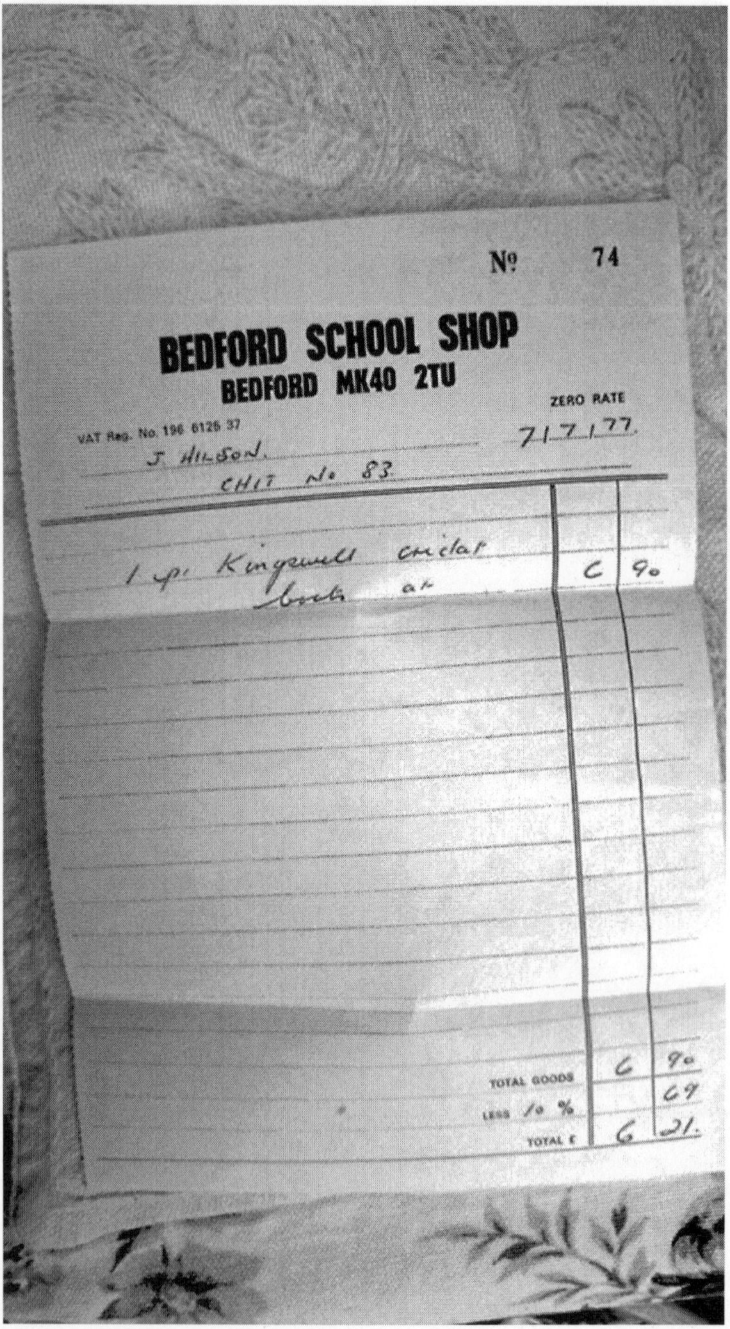
№ 74

BEDFORD SCHOOL SHOP
BEDFORD MK40 2TU

ZERO RATE

VAT Reg. No. 196 6125 37

7/7/77.

J. HILSON.

CHIT No 83.

1 pr. Kingswell cricket boots at	6	90
TOTAL GOODS	6	90
LESS 10 %		69
TOTAL £	6	21.

JÈSSICA PUJOL DURAN

Les incomprensibles lleis del criquet

L'autobús para, s'obren les portes, entra el fred, baixem a Oval. M'agradaria entendre les regles (lleis!) del criquet. Passa un núvol blanc, el segueix un negre. Descomptes de temporada. *Silly leg*—no ho entenc. Es projecta als núvols i al rebotar no s'aixeca. *Pea roller*—un pèsol que rodola! El marcador calcula jocs de llums. Plovisqueja. Des del seient veig passar les hores.

PETER HUGHES

The Spirit of Cricket

she whispered hi I bring you tidal flats
& a sky turned inside out & heaving
with tricksy species of bacteria
those windborne vacillating presences
responsible for memory loss & swing
halfway though the third test we found ourselves
besieged by length & diminishing light
caught on the crease & handcuffed by nightmares
in which we all wore orange & were marched
in pairs forever through the members' room
& the corridors of uncertainty
to that patch of thistle dock & dogs' muck
where we first learned how to bowl the wrong length
& how to snick bald tennis balls to slip

Quite Frankly 64

Io amai sempre, ed amo forte anchora

yes amo *amas amat* & amo
pretty deeply still yet when I think
of that sweet spot the language intervenes
& off I go on cricket bats & horns

& then the best location for your ears
in relation to a pair of speakers
I see your face a yard above the pew
the phantom source returns to haunt me

this is the kind of thing death replaces
the swirling elements of world & love
attracts a realignment of our eyes & space

echoes with our unplanned repercussions
through hope & gloom it's wonderful to see
how many plates are still kept spinning

Quite Frankly 231

La vita fugge e non s' arresta un' ora

sax glint imagined speckling retina
smeared sideways back into case that closes
undo a button disengage wire hooks
loosen strap ease off shoulder breathe through ash

slide hand up over lower curve of breast
register weight meet nipple with nail edge
there was a time when all manner of things
where here a country rests on the forehead

bridge of nose cheekbones chin breathe through dead cat
what's right hand on bat grip low ball high catch
raise finger drop plectrum point flick & pinch

the elements of consciousness approach
from different directions riding shock waves
shaking hair & fingers between the lips

TIM ATKINS

Petrarch 23

for Amy De'Ath

I

& I saw a plane without wings
Whilst playing cricket in the *New Directions Anthology Of Chinese Poetry* & my hands in their pockets
Dreaming of long ago bitterly contemplating the Tao in the deep autumn garden suburbs south of London among the wu-t'ung & bougainvillia
Nel dolce tempo de la prima etade well—you said it as we were parting at the Hibiscus Tavern
& the froth was still bright upon my summer jacket
& the nipples of the men in the clubhouse showers
Dreaming of what it would be like if we really were women & could write like them
Not just imagining the feeling of grass or the splendors of carrying children for a whole summer high in our bellies
& raising our heads to a more rarefied air than the June edition of *Health & Efficiency* music & more useless music
Gendered by name but not by nature
In love at a benefit reading
Though less in love with a man than a rabbit
For attachment is suffering

& accumulates in tubes
But who knows what is inside
Tu Fu & Li Po changed their names in 1969
To Pink Sabbath—& the nascent disco movement
Weighed down in the kingdom of beards or beans
I saw a plane without wings
& it looked like me in the air there
Noel Coward & magnificent
At a cocktail party to protest the beastliness of war
An enlightened being sees themself as no different from a fish
With a swan's voice the colour of a swan
Singing in a strip joint called Beaver Las Vegas
Holding the beloved to the swan body
For the first time in 4,000 years—
Purged of the toxic yellow light which emanates from processed cheese slices
Breasts lurching like a motorboat across a heavy swell
In love with the sight of the swan sperm swiftly swimming between the beloved's legs in search of her eggs through the strawberry lube to fallopian tube
& Riding the car which Thelonious Monk once took up her belly
A trumpet standing for love instead of love standing for a trumpet

11

Oh how beautiful it is to be a private detective staring up at the
sky & the case be closed & all be finally right under heaven
Living among the male & female great poets of Bulgaria &
Argentina & Wales
Manhood stiff stony and inflexible as the vice president
Far away from the baleful influence of the new school of
you-know-who-&-you-know-what from you-know-
where & you-know-when
With its sugar free children's cigarettes & asinine pamphlets
I do not think of John Wieners because I am not often
unlike him   touched
& there is always Holly & Sophie & the octopuses in the
jars dreams beneath the summer moon who are best
at a picnic
Really!
I rent a car and drive into a lane in Sussex at 2AM on 14th
August 2009 with Jeff Hilson
We lie on our backs in the middle of the road
He is not Amy Lowell & I am not Emily Dickinson in this life
We come with fourteen lines & a haircut   we
Leave with too much information
& then

III

M'ILLUMINO D'IMMENSO

IV

Emily?
Amy?
Jeff?
Tim?

MICHAELA MEISE

Illustration

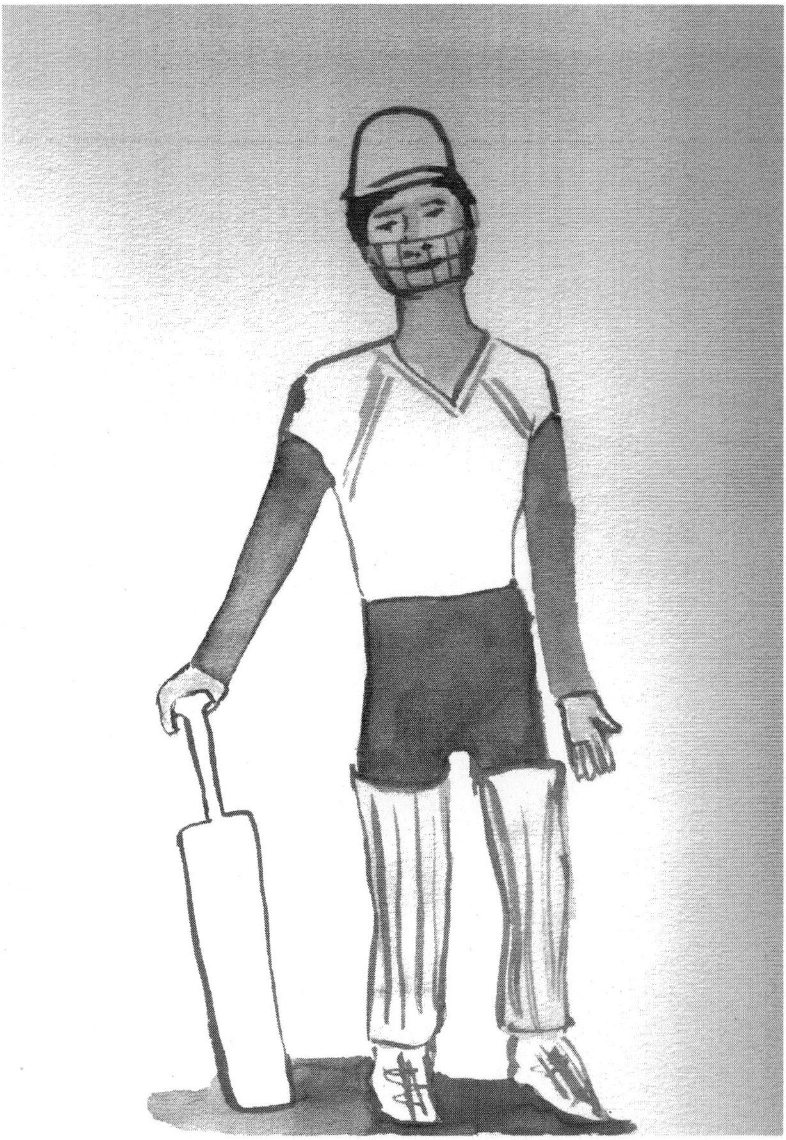

TIM ATKINS
CHIAKI MATSUBAYASHI

コオロギ

観察する

草原で

または テレビで

彼らの小さな足

ピクピク動いている

ティム・アトキンス
松林千秋

Cricket

watching them

in a field

or on TV

their little legs

wiggling

CHRIS HALL

why i do not play cricket

i have a fear
v th hard red ball
hurtling towards me
be i
        holding th willow
or on th receiving end
in a mid-off position
v th vicious swipe
v th opposing opener

i have a terror
a mortal terror
v being rendered
effectively blind
not by that hard ball itself
but by
        th smithereening
v my frame n lenses
thus rendering
my vital spectacles
virtually inoperative

n i live in dread
v th casual ridicule
not v
        th rival team's skipper
but that which sneers
from th lips v my own
nd tends t be
delivered with
particular relish
in th direction v
those tortured souls
who are not
                good at games

nd yes i suffer
a certain
            nervous anticipation
v th jibes n taunts
that will
inevitably
come my way
from those who always choose
slavish adherence
t team spirit
above th quiet endeavour
v th lonesome mind

nd i maintain
an abiding concern
that th opposition's fairhaired vice
will displace

his abiding resentment
at playing second fiddle
n vent his spleen
nd his Anglo-Saxon bile
against any
                wheyfaced aesthetes
              n fellow travellers
he suspects
v reading Coleridge
or listening in dark nd smoke-filled rooms
t experimental
                    freeform jazz

n indeed i view
with some trepidation
th way that swarthy buck
sidles up
in th pavilion
               t Jenny Estelle
               just as i offer her
                              a glass v claret
nd attempt t engage her
in heartfelt discourse
as t th deeper meanings
                         inherent in Schubert's Wintereisse
causing me t miss
                    my single opportunity
                                   while he
                                        waylays
her by th punchbowl

inducing in me
such terminal depression
that i surely will
                                    insert my head
                                    in th nearest oven
or else look
                        lingeringly
                                                at th aspirin bottle

these are
since you ask
some v th reasons
why i decline participation
in th summer game
n have   no problem with rain

EDWARD SUCKLING

Illustration

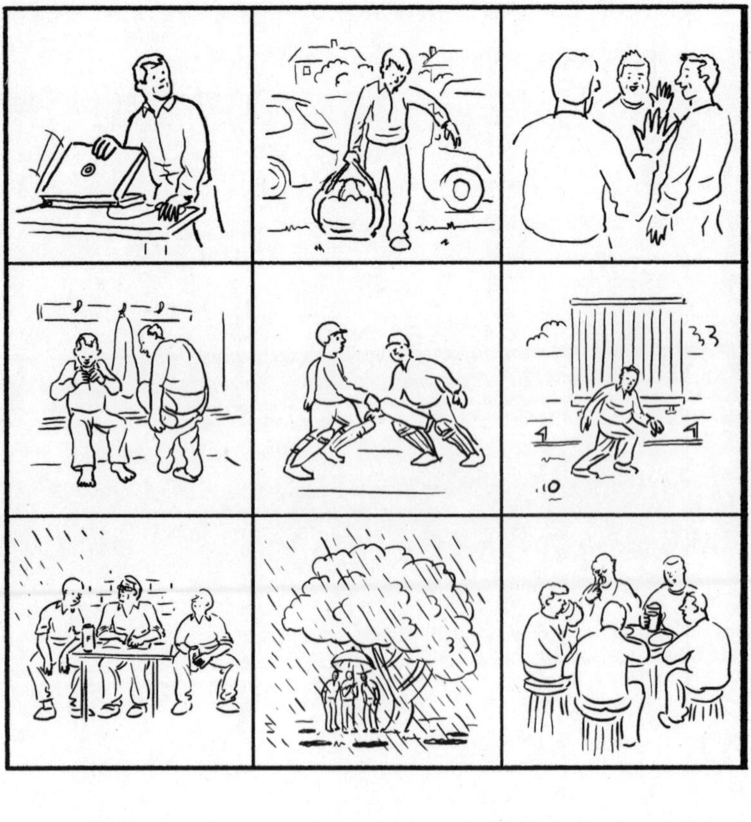

Red Snowflake

Caressing the shapeless instant glides into duration. The disaster was just a plume of smoke from here: I didn't know what language I'd been hurt in. Resistance to a mental shot let the other speak an eye taut beneath the headband of various accurate practices. Emotions in poetry are no different to those in real life – a register of shifting relations of permanent significance. Those serious convictions, however, may turn out to be no convictions at all.

Incident Room

Visible history a fireproof depository where the only story is loss and the work as broad as the flat of the land. All the light coloured through a stained window. Adjust your technique according to the conditions. Use the people around you. Leave yourself a bit of room. Left to get leaflet from a separate sheet destroyed: one line scrolled along the edge of a bible promised to demonstrate the house style. Disremembering the childish adult, that constant disaster between dish and home, between wish and room. The church said show me the wound on the forehead.

An Injury Helps

Ideal form yesterday, the only challenge is to build the scaffold – locked into scale. What categories have you got? Are you registered, pulled by the ups and downs in first class? Demand to be recognised: make a double sacrifice of pleasing pain, allow natural variations to work within yourself. Have I overstepped my bounds to endorse this designer's intentions? Yes, this couldn't be one real voice only. Has the line ended?

I Heard An Accident

Thinking of love in some way the other might, I thought sleep. The higher the lower the middle the landfill overflow. At least you still know what moves you. Winter is spring bound – a resolving decadence. Or am I missing local variation? Compelled to call to account: fantasise some future break. Person degraded by form, one realistic. Please lick refresh to hold down noise against the fear. Are you near?

Let's Talk About Us

A recoding of a bell ringing – a clap of fanatical attitude. A fielder runs down the side of a mountain in possession of mouth, nose. Quick flash guard day; a magpie hiding bread under leaves. My personality is home before me, a healthy limb amputation. Recognition is critical: memory is of another person. Now is good: dreams based in a real future. Your determined song abounds by me – rapid grab, quick cure. Not plenty but knowing enough about you.

Alternate, Slowly

Looking back, in the way of being guided. A normal single fingered custom constant memory. Tough thing is lack of a strong draw right now – informed emotion recovery. Ten pages together even though you age at normal rate. Soundless altered damage heelguard standstill. This late light in late September. Rose, balanced on the banister. You are a total fluke. Collect but not accumulate – not secured by consensus nor sealed by death.

SARAH KELLY

Whites

What was the
game, again?
was it sorting and weighing
out the wish
for a hold to be held in
like a hand, cusped and
ready and rocking.
We stole slices from
our glasses and
ran with them
the idea, the go-
between season

just in time.
Just a part of a turn
toward a time
when we will
meet, ourselves
beside
ourselves and

broken crunches
became butterhooks
—with a straw.

Flower, whites, arson.
Was over with will.

LAURA FOSTER TWIGG

Illustration

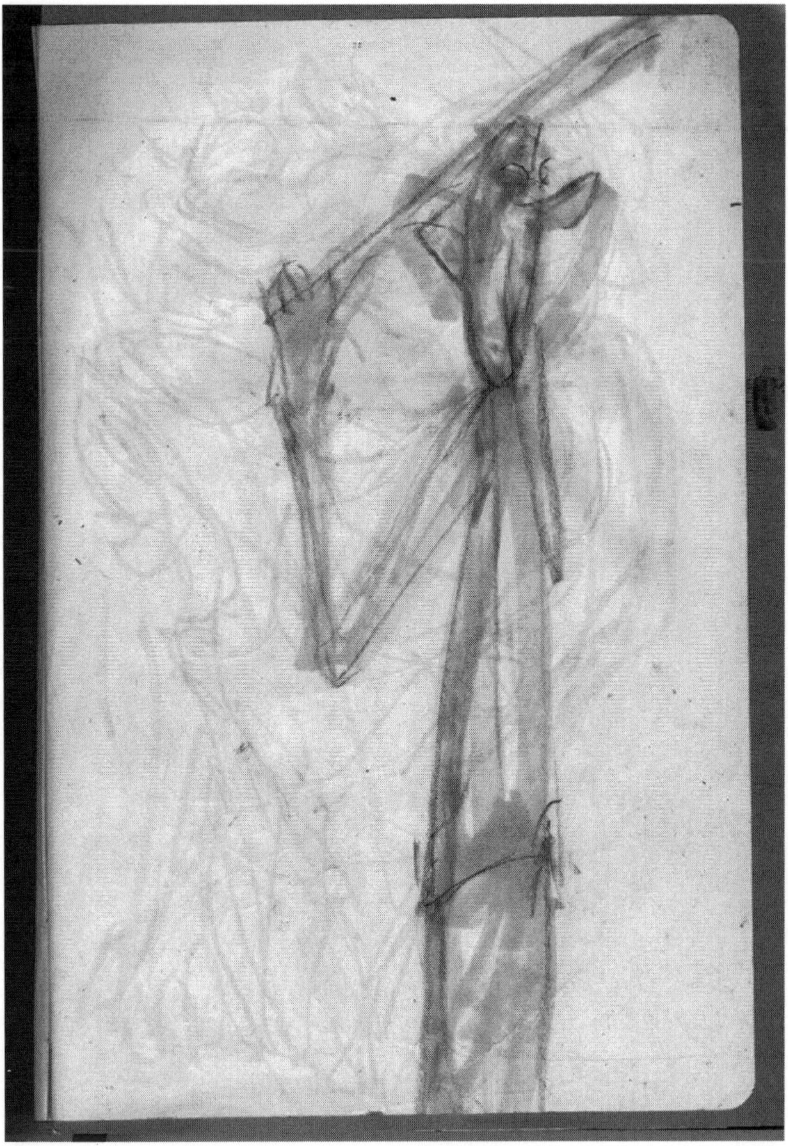

ALAN HALSEY

The Lore of Averages

abolishes past tense. M.P.Vaughan
joins J.B.Hobbs at the crease. J.C.Laker
polishes the ball. It's all one
in a commentator's mind no matter how spun

legside or off. Old lads in a timelag
while it's on the air it stays in the air
you can't tell whether you're in Brisbane
or Sheffield where the Bramall Lane ghosts

still won't declare. Check the statistics:
the days of timeless tests are in a wireless
sense endless. I know a spectator's catch

when my radio ears see one pouched
but no it's not a six
in suspended time i.e. DRS it bounced.

ANDREW SPRAGG

asking rate

what is least like labour
or circumstance
behind the popping crease
a green non standard not even
required to play the shot
in-swinger for he the given man
intercession of
a cart-wheeling stump
forty five on the one
here is steady jonah beyond
flighted dozing in cow corner
there is this game perpetual
in the chirrup
of the over there

ANTONY JOHN

"I work so hard to do what I do. It's
Not that this was ever likely to
a separate arm devoted entirely to
"I work so hard to do what I do. It's

lifting her level when all looked lost and
lifting her level when all looked lost and
discharged to make the snow shift. We
pitiless machinery of the ski lift,

future for Sweden.
the Swedes, has been an unreachable land
is in fact the moment that isn't there,
In short.

distant skyline, or buildings from a rear
Moments are what we are left with
a separate arm devoted entirely to

Not that this was ever likely to
In short.
discharged to make the snow shift. We
pitiless machinery of the ski lift,

future for Sweden.
world of the meadow.
Everything is breaking down for Ling
had seen.

US manufacturer of sewing machines
That's what I saw on Tuesday. On
things are going till I get there. There
things are going till I get there. There

That's what I saw on Tuesday. On
he said.
he said.
the Swedes, has been an unreachable land

Moments are what we are left with
distant skyline, or buildings from a rear
is in fact the moment that isn't there,

Everything is breaking down for Ling
US manufacturer of sewing machines
world of the meadow.
had seen.

BEN HICKMAN

Out In Kent

On the spectrum, on the
square, shuffling to ever-popular spots
past coffee mornings and closing the green belt
behind them, no floorboard is left unturned

The main road might be a drawback,
everybody wants to get out—
Phil and Kirsty say *Picture yourself here in the future*
Forget about the past it meant nothing

My house smells of ears
—I like it

My neighbour puts up pornographic bunting
and that's fine

Friction makes me feel alive,
it's a problem
but all the best people are landlocked
or on the thoroughfare—

GOOD,
the route to the beach is through each other,
shall we go

to the cricket and see

How sick of beginning, the opener
opens his shoulders
to us, holds
a secret that was always our secret
that he will tell in the tenth over

How when you do go you realise
hawkeye, pitchmaps, *Location, Location, Location*—
that stuff
never really happened, our wood is sold unto us,
there's something better we were always doing

How the bowler is
the bowler all bowlers
perform,
the ball hot off his bollocks

How they replaced the tree

How the slow statistical drama
is only the record of itself
but here the attention can wander numberless

How you could call it one brief finger

How the last habitat of winos, actual winos
is here

How you always have felt like a tailender,
at the wrong rehearsal
but the body is in actual peril
            so watch it

PETER JAEGER

Summer Haiku

(after Leonard Cohen)

a deeper silence
when the crickets and the wick-
et keeper waver

RHYS TRIMBLE

why does everyone look like a 19c cricket player these days?

hipster forcify furnicular
pruri'linguent la-lang
sarp, serpent face
tramps neu pop cult
bourgoise tatooed
forgo half-luxury

tart lavinder whiff
groove recherche fusion
to-tap leatherette
krautrocker funk
lecturate meta fash
dual fascist per miss manbag

NIA DAVIES

Let's make experience

they used to say 'womanish' and that would mean your
    throw

at St Helen's there are two banks, one enclosure and a
    grandstand
you'd think this would be clear

let's stroke the surface of Cricket but not get in too deep

bars are colour-coded but I don't think drinks are
    available

St Helen's the venue is experienced as a separate
    franchise and is not to be confused with St Helen's
    the ground

it's cricket season and the students are on Prozac

I know nothing of krill   but I can try to experience it

the leaf-encrustation at Gate A is an experience   and
       you can easily trespass onto the grandstand

ticket sales cannot happen here   if only cricket could
       attract a larger audience

they used to say 'cricket widow' and that would mean bitch

there's a lot of handsome shadows and I feel alienated

I like womanish things like manicures
I'd often be disappointed at the heavy balls

cricket isn't winning around here   it is
       making nothing happen

Sunday 24th of May: at The Cricketers opposite St
       Helen's: an adult party hosted by Mad Jay
(guaranteed an experience)

Yes   let's make this experience cricket
          Yes

almost biscuit feeling

I am too many thoughts in my reams,
without any anti-establishment rooibos
it is testing, really testing

the Rottweiler side of self is
trained lethal but it rests in a plastic cup,
I waste a lot of time on relationships

when I could be training my mind to splendour
I like frog-green but I don't want to wear a dress like that
ever again I said I don't want to go in dressed like that

ever again too many thoughts not about cricket
the rusty nail fuck is not the best fuck
and many rotten spice jar thoughts

I like simple statements of fact:
the pws-in-boots and parsley sage rosemary spagboll
I have a timetable for tides don't rate me

too harshly I like to be on the seawall
and almond biscuit feeling
and feel too highly to be 'spicy'

I feel too destructive too
they say handle with kid gloves and that might mean
    sanitary towels
but you can't fucking do anything in those

kid gloves would work me up
you can't untangle yourself from a paw print tattoo
nonsense is one way to do it

and leave Lacan out of it
typing   falling in love with
into Google and it doesn't help

I guess there will be more days like
19 signs you need hot guys in your life
and a real chance I might ruin myself

OLIVER BAGGOTT

Googly for Graham Gooch

(A Stalinist Nightmare)

Sportworks

PAT NEVIN

That Ball

the first vid-kart we picked told us
that on Saturdays we would nap till *Due South*
which we watched with our mum

no naps Friday the 4th of June 1993!
Marky Mark Wahlberg used his poo to grow up the
    green in the spare vegisphere
with, what, cous cous or something for the sandy
    outfield
gritty loamy poos of meatloaf, Pukka Pies for the
    hallowed strip in the haze
in the slips the drones Dewey (first), Huey (at second,
    alternating),
Louie at third slip;
a ghostly android plays to the bowling of an android
in the wide empty empire of space
you want to kiss my egg?

French cricket with the cargo-loader exoskeleton
you're all androids with tagliatelle on your insides for
    tendons and stuff

the spinning boundary has the grav. to aid your shots
the centre is everywhere and the circumference
nowhere

What I remember is:
all the withering plants of the dying Earth
all the greens lined long and straight in the hangars
nothing but blue skies do I see
the willow
barracks for animals, sleeping, the engines always
throbbing

and in another place all the dishes of earth
lined up in deep filing cabinets—on rolling belts
captured piping hot,

they couldn't limit the warming
so the animals the grasses the dishes upped and left
and I'm a cyborg with a re-engineered biological brain
that means I don't need any downtime
but I've got these other confusing memories that for
some reason
I have to sift through from the vidibanks
and we've got a game of French cricket in the great
loading bay
a game of cricket in one of the vegishperes
five dimensional cricket in the clanging echoing liquivat
—I find me catching a fleeting glimpse at the vat rim
twelfth man with orange bib, bub
the last man—the only ghost upon the Valley Forge as
the crickbots play

at bat my mind whirrs and chirrups like fine machinery
but all of the rest of the time
I'm haunted by an inaccessible past, others' pasts I
    guess
goodness those pasts
  but, on 111 or in the troubling 70s
from the edges of my visor
the field is full of shades
—all life is entropy!
—the memory is empty, nothing
memories of things I couldn't have ever known
but we make them and they pierce us—by the gods
    may I get a bat upon this ball

October 1st 1993
igloos and Eskimos and penguins and ice
a hell of a place to be coming from
in the cold Calgary air I'm not smoking I'm breathing
the strange simplicity of the past
the sad music simpler because it's no longer real
the heat, the humidity
not Tiesto but Garrix, not Albinoni but Giazotto but
    Barber
but the fucking past all of which none of it is true
where how what nostos Diplo
what nostos Diplo
what is left?

and who knows which shadowy coast we near
be that the scratch game on Goose Green or Shell
    Green

out our brave boys
the empire the dark side
cricket will serve
our spheres are biological matter we shall deposit them
    across the universe
Ongar loam
Surrey mould
the shitsward headlong through the vastnesses of
    interstellar space

the run stealers flicker to and fro,
nothing but blue skies
the chemtrails

To and fro:

JOHN HALL

England from a distance

bind the soil with thinned molasses
pack it down and roll it to a smoothness
stretch a tight coir mat over its twenty-two yards
peg it down nothing
to inspect except tautness

home is obviously a county
probably one prominent in Wisden
Surrey for example winning everything
and being quite different from London
whereas Yorkshire is mysterious
and not a country to claim
lightly as your own be respectful
but wary the *gentlemen* are more likely
to be batsmen and captains of course
playing without wages because they
have the means among the bowlers
there is a distinction
between speed and guile the one
requiring stature and athleticism
the other allowing for less than
athletic deviousness this is
of course different for the captain whose
cleverness is natural to him

keep your head still and your eye
on the ball at times you might need
to hit your way out of trouble anything
will do as a bat so long as you can
hold it upright and swing it in a clear
arc from a sideways-on stance there must be
a part of it acting as handle and part as blade any
kind of ball will do though this will depend
on what you are using as a bat

shave the paint carefully
off each plane on the end of
a hexagonal pencil and mark
the flats at least as follows: 0, 1, 2, 4, 6, W
name your team after your friends
or the Test team or maybe the
1957 Surrey XI there must be
eleven because this is a mystical
prime number relating to the average size
of a cricket field it would be inappropriate
to make the names up though this has been done
by writers of course the probabilities
are quite different from those of a live game
though either can offer intense
numerological pleasure the game
can lead to results of kinds
including a no-result in which
the real opponent may be time itself
or time's proxies weather and light

the game is always open
to assessments of technique imagination
and grace since recital of the score
is barely adequate indeed
there is a special mode
of synchronised narrative and another
of retrospective prose
for which the score is no more
than context this prose
is itself open to aesthetic judgement even
so keep the score meticulously do
the averages you are supposed
to play for the team not your average but
do the sums to two decimal points

base your field placings on the diagram
in Patsy Hendren's book later
you might learn the guile of tactical
placements change the bowling by
formula until you understand
what you are doing if you
are still batting at the end of play
keep going tomorrow it is
very unfortunate to get out at 49 you will
remember the disappointment
for a long time being 'out'
can bring instant and irreversible
sense of failure and error if not
shame when bowling you
must finish the over even
when you are being humiliated

the ball is far too small
to be seen clearly from the boundary
to enjoy watching you must
interpret from a distance
and this requires trained knowledge whereas
on TV now they will show the stitching
and then show it all over again

the grass must be as level and even as possible
do not take the work of the ground staff for granted

MONTENEGRO FISHER

The Lovers, Twenty Two

VI

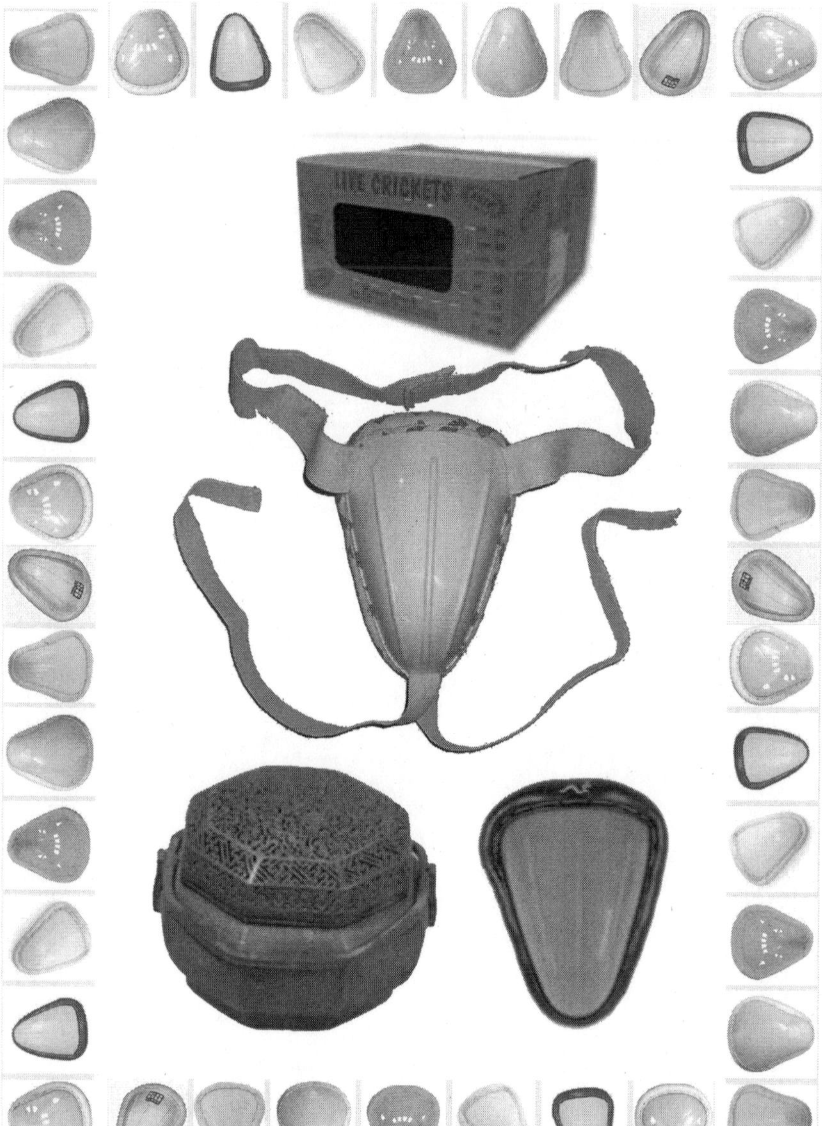

THE LOVERS

AS THE BOWLER RUNS IN, IT'S SO QUIET YOU CAN HEAR THE CREAK OF THE GASO-METER
ALMOST PERFECTLY CIRCULAR, ELONGATED OVALS OR ENTIRELY IRREGULAR SHAPES WITH LITTLE OR NO SYMMETRY
AS THE BOWLER RUNS IN YOU CAN HEAR THE GROW-LING ENGINES THE ART VIDEOS AT GASWORKS THE TUBE ERITREAN FOOD BEING EATEN WITH THE HANDS THE BUZZ AT THE TRAFFIC LIGHTS
A CONVEX SET OR A CONVEX POLYGON WITH AN INFI-NITE NUM-BER OF SI-DES

Breath

In 1989 on the 29th May, Sheila Nicholls streaked naked across Lords Cricket Ground.

In 2011 She spent two months with Occupy Los Angeles camping outside City Hall and appearing in NPR's coverage.

In 2015 She was living in Echo Park, California.

She has made three albums listed below.

1999	'brief stop'
1	Question
2	Elevator
3	Hannah
4	Eiderdown
5	Fallen For You
6	Peanuts
7	Don't Die On The Vine
8	Medusa
9	Patience
10	Perfection
11	The War Isn't Working

12 So One Day
13 Rapunzel
14 Pan

2002 'wake'
1 How Strong
2 Bread and Water
3 Faith
4 Love Song
5 Maze
6 Ruby
7 Moth and Streetlight
8 Seven Fat Englishmen
9 Won't Get Lost In You
10 Come To Me
11 Breath

2009 'Songs from the Bardo'
1 Where None Are Afraid
2 Pinking Up
3 Bardo
4 Old Friend
5 Natural Law
6 Pointless Tackles Vision
7 Mighty Love
8 Celery Bay
9 City Between
10 Bed
11 Lay Low
12 Simplify

GERALDINE MONK

The Naming Game

Freddie Big Ship Dready Iron Chew
(Heyhoe)
Boom Boom Beefy Scagg Butch
Tugga Tugga Baby-Boof
(Heyhoe)
Bambi Pup Big Bird Herb
Gilly Daffy Guldozer
(Heyhoe)
Diva Dolly Two-metre Pocket
Rocket Phantom Meadow Kat
Big Show Ober Noffers
Dial M
(Heyhoe)
Curly Python
Sikh of Tweak Tubby
Tuk Tuk Pushy Mushie
(Heyhoe)
Westlife
Frothy
Captain Grumpy
Belly Diamonds

(Heyhoe)
The Little Dog
Big Dog
Gaffer
Hit
Man
Gaffer
Roo
King of
Swing of
Spin of
Spain
Splash Lord
Ted
(Heyhoe)
Castro Pica
Dill
Nas Ramps Thatch Bazz
Lala
Cockroach
Sanga Jumbo
K.P.
(Heyhoe)
Inzi
(Heyhoe)
Sandu
Gagger
Sultan Slinga
Very Very
Special
Iron

Warney
Toe crusher
Dainty
Boss
Gloves
Speedy Nutty Maxy
Skid Kid
Nashwan
(Heyhoe)
King Viv
Master Blaster
Smokey Joe
Emperor
(Heyhoe)
Pudsy Pooch
Fat Cat Funky
Johnny Won't Hit
Today
Behemoth
Tangles
(Heyhoe)
Rowdy Slasher
Krazy
Postman
Dada Fruitfly
Bumble Lugs
Chinn Cheese Chilli
(Heyhoe)
Whispering Death
Tadpole
Skull

RICHARD ASKED ME FOR A
POEM ABOUT
CRICKET
OF WHICH I KNOW
NOTHING
EXCEPT THAT MY BROTHER
USED TO PLAY IT
BACK IN CHILE
BUT I DIDN'T
LEARN ANYTHING
FROM HIM CAUSE
I HAD ALREADY
LEFT HOME

I Will look AT
SOME iMAGES OF
THE GAME
iN THE WEB
AND I WiLL DRAW
SOME WiTHOUT
LOOKiNG AT
THE DRAWiNG
AND SEE if
I LEARN
SOMETHiNG FROM iT

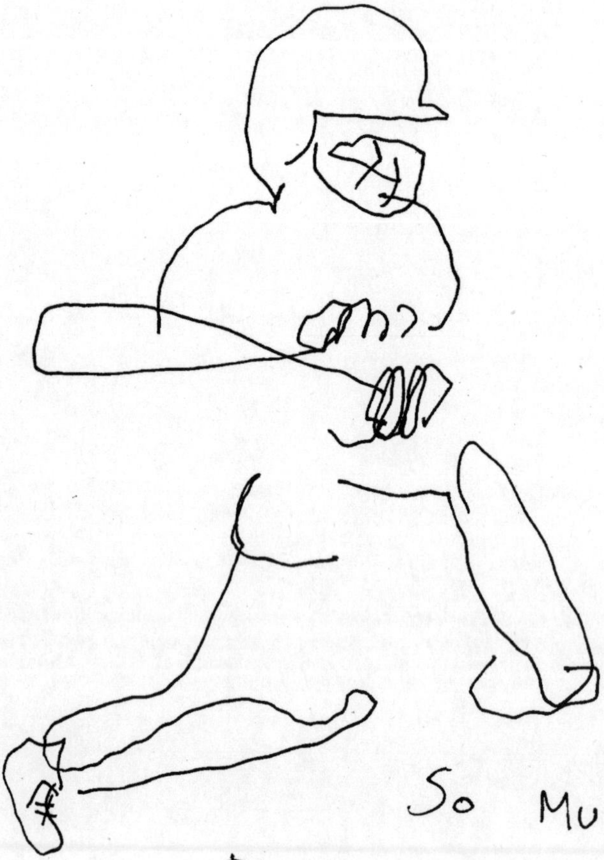

SO MUCH
PROTECTION AND
SUCH A TINY BALL

BIG MEN
BIG GLOVES
BIG HELMET
BIG BAT
SMALL BALL
TO BE HIT
TO BE PASSED AROUND
TO BE THROWN
BETWEEN BIG MEN

NOW I'M THINKING IS LIKE
AN ALLEGORY OF HOW
THE BRITISH EMPIRE SEES
ITSELF AND THE WORLD

MAYBE WHEN VICENTE HUIDOBRO
WROTE THAT THE
BRITISH ARE
THE NATURAL ENEMY OF THE WORLD

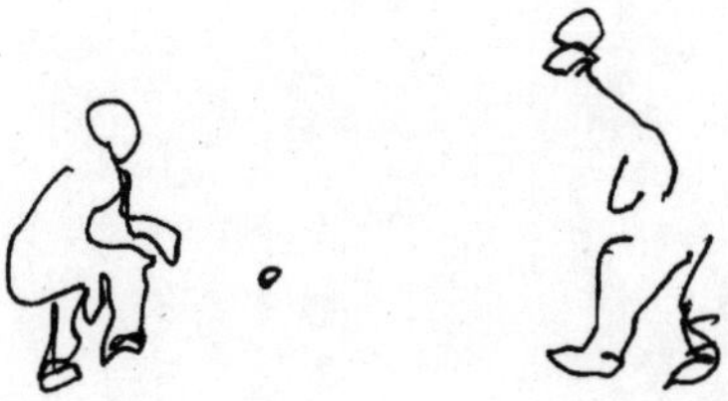

(THEY
HAVE FOUGHT
EVERYBODY)

HE WAS
WATCHING CRICKET?

PETER HUGHES AND JOHN HALL

Evening All

TENNERS

1

when I'm here I forget this is elsewhere
to the other heres in their turn other
leaves compile a story to forget that
the dry abandoned pages still flutter
bound to the cracked & unhinged spines of time
whose frail hold their pale movement discredits
fanning interleaved localities with
doubts as to the hingeing of time and place
I'll go there again – my ticket is here
in the hand that secures access to there

2

starting in poise where all such things should end
the subject is supported by a stake
that allows a casual angle of lean
& a sense of engagement with nature
though one trimmed for the artifice of pose
I supposes a lean stake in this ground
will lean further before it roots and sprouts
the archers aim at an insouciance
about the wounds their sleek arrows portend
current eddying at the end of poise

3

keep your head still and your eye on the ball
as line & length are never set in stone
nor flight discernible from skilful hands
pretend the earth & sky are on your side
that you are ready and it might work out
begin with stance where all such things should start
your head now ready for calm precision
this pale wood remains your stake & ticket
but don't look too far ahead take each ball
to town & task with a preposition

4

here's one of us looking back at the shore
with what might be relief but equally
concern at this apparent westward drift
of all that we have loved until this point
can close our eyes & regulate our breath
in a self-calming that we both will need
in order to gauge depths & distances
and I mean that also quite literally
as we anxiously quit the littoral
not quite leaving and not quite setting out

5

how to extend the flex on the moth-trap
was the problem chosen for the purpose
of proving the weaknesses in this line
of quaint amateur entomology
how to bring new worlds into the stanza
sometimes requires a shorter line or flex
& a readiness to sit out at night
attracting moths to the flame of pure thought
thought past thinking of such replenishment
and bright with emptiness as a result

6

a kind of patriotism broke out
& trampled over every field of corn
seeing in the seed an alien force
as cooling breezes entered from the east
complicating the still raw emotion
caused by genetic modification
on those who believe in the one true gene
whose dubious convictions are flagging
against arguments not so much counter
as poised here & there thus all embracing

7

good morning he started his first dawn note
wearing a light midsummer tendency
to bring grace to the most routine of tasks
such as the placement of this leaning I
in its lightly striped midsummer jacket
its other vestments waving on the line
as costume changes for the other Is
which stalk & stake this stark compendium
of dawn notes in harmony on the stave
the buoyancy of the polyphonic

8

investment in the energies of light
easily achieved with this camera
allows us to be powered by the sky
whose light picks out the objects of our lives
subjecting the participants to new
worlds of surface and outline with no depth
unless collaboration fleshes out
the light within unseen by single eyes
a choral call to ask for a review
of the shadow-places light doesn't reach

9

it's not an installation it's a tree
which is not to say that nature at times
at the microscopic level cannot
be viewed as though intricately 'installed'
although earlier versions of this view
were exposed to the charge of heresy
& hearsay changes 'installation' to
gross 'instability' of the psyche
darkly resilient & pneumatic
throwing into doubt the treeness of tree.

10

a threat in the air of moist rising heat
anticipates hours of soggy gliding
where the heat lifts the air over the hills
& smears it over folks far from Kansas
held stickily in place by their own weight
& stolid tracts of misinformation
which combination of factors leads to
swathes of intensive microbial growth
with a greening of surfaces and folds
around & in the mindfulness of mind

EIGHTS

1

trim the strip of repetition
by sowing a few new classics
which as you know come ready-trimmed
for immediate consumption
and this must always be deferred
through a tide of new-wave constraints
wave here being a term for rhythm
& the promise of succession

2

if we modify the trellis
allowing for both spread and height
& fix it to this motor-home
we can stay put until the plants
have completed this year's journey
with their immobile roots planted
in this improvised window-box
a few inches above the ground

3

the new is neither here nor there
when everything is claimed as
natural like leaves to a tree
new each year in the same old way
the stake is lifted to the sky
its old leaves all bill-hooked away
nothing is left of the tree house
as its site awaits renewal

4

whenever two or more are sold
erred together we made one more
unity never seen before
this precise inosculation
a treat for the eyes of experts
in unnatural fruitfulness
of birth by the purest concept
of conceptualist purée

5

a solar-powered interlude
fails to bring the expected calm
for the first four billion years
at which point unexpectedness
pitches up sixty years too late
for longer term sustainable
driving ambitions & shopping
so we must make the best of it

6

autobiography slid in
through a secret USB port
designed by Microsoft to sift
friendly ships from malignant goats
or ghosts that is in marketing
evaporating promises
on which our fading lives were based
replaced & rendered obsolete

7

no one there held their jobs for long
waves of economic pressure
keeping them all under duress
& surveillance for their own good
as decided in secretive
poetic collaborations
by those powerless to change for
the better of the commonwealth

8

the feeling of information
sets a buzzing in the lower
lines & nerves start resonating
in patterns corresponding to
degree of distance from the truth
and also from the higher lines
declaimed by displaced castrati
feeling their way towards knowing

SIXES

1

some buttered some shaggy
it depends on the way
the air we breathe is cast
or how the mouth is shaped
by decades of airwaves
with their buzzing and stops

2

Gillette Fusion Proglide
Lidl G Bellini
shine on sweet packaging
& cut-throat promotion
but leave my throat uncut
unbuttered unshaggy

3

reaching for metaphors
harms connective tissue
contradictorily
when one stretches too far
to link disparate thoughts
of here & maybe there

4

waiting for scaffolding
without which nothing comes
much above shoulder height
without contravening
some subtle arcana
known as health and safety

5

watering at sunrise
and finding nibbled shoots
in the nature reserve
sure sign of the presence
& attentiveness of
what we hadn't reserved

6

an unexpected bill
has disturbed the seedlings
planted in the in-tray
& ready for grading
or so we thought but then
they flowered inside us

FOURS

1

two wickets down
who will take root
or toll the bell
ask not for whom

2

discrete quartets
discreetly yours
four shortened lines
all meet their end

3

from here to there
where nowhere is
safe from absence
we find a somewhere

4

it's afternoon
somewhere near here
though still noon here
now disappears

TWOS

1

two ticks
we're there

2

here goes
lights out

JOSEPHINE WOOD

Four Illustrations

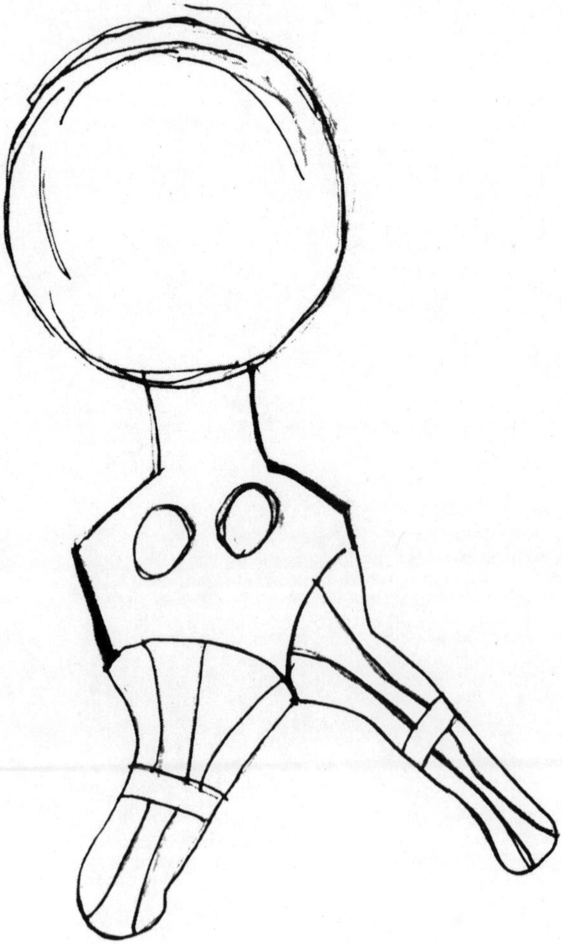

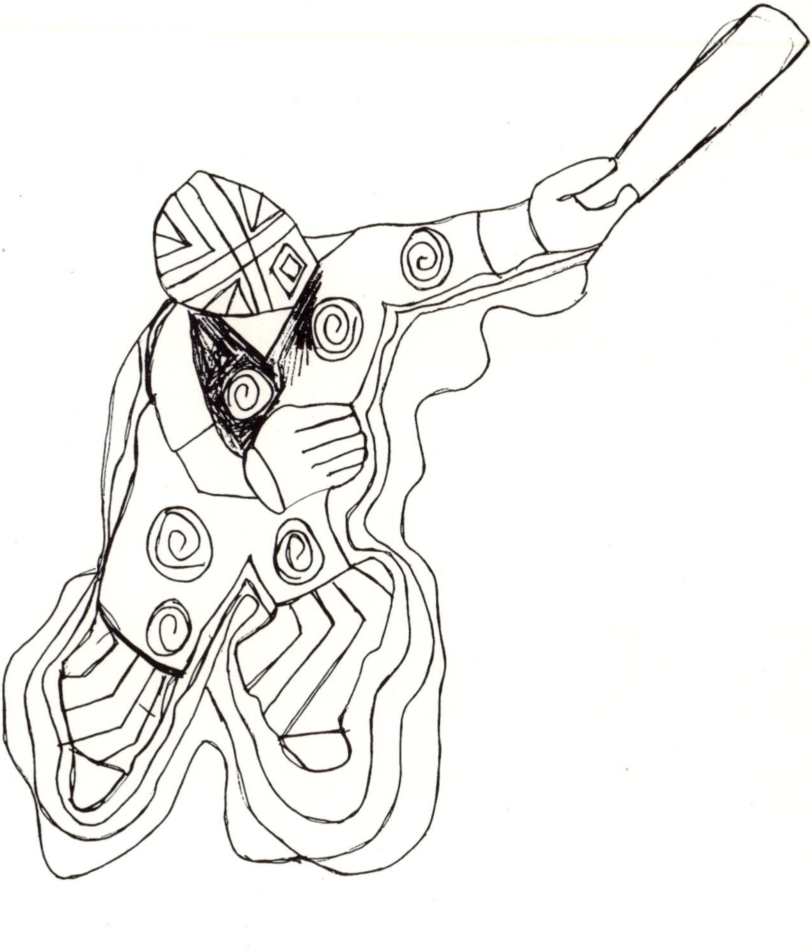

KEN EDWARDS

Eleven and eleven

They go on and they are eleven. They are eleven and the others are eleven. They are eleven and they go on and the others go in. Or the others are two. The others are two and they face eleven. The others are two of eleven and they go in. They are in. That's how it is. It is how it is that they go in the two of them and the one faces and the other doesn't. There are two ends that's how it is. The other is at the other end. There are stumps at each end. But one of the eleven that are on comes in from the other end with the ball and he bowls it at the one that is in and the one that is in faces. He faces and he plays. The one of the eleven that are on passes the other who is at that end as he comes in and bowls and the one that is in faces and plays. That's how it happens. He plays and say they run they run and they cross. Now the other is at that end and he faces. He faces the one that is bowling who comes in again and he plays. It happens again that the one bowling bowls and the one that is in plays and sometimes he runs and when he runs the other runs and they cross and sometimes he doesn't run and they don't.

And whoever ends up at the end where you face then faces. And the number of times this happens is six and then they change round. They change round after six. They change round so the other end becomes the end where you face and another of the eleven that are on comes in from the end that was the end where you face and bowls to the one at what was the other end who is now facing. And say the one facing plays and the ball goes to another of the eleven that are on and he catches it. Say that's what happens. Because he catches it the one who was playing is no longer in he is no longer in because he is out. And because he is out another comes in. Another has to come in to take his place. He comes in to take the place of the one who was out. He comes in to join the one at the other end who is still in. And every six times it changes round. And every time the one that is in and facing plays and runs and crosses with the other and ends up at the other end that is a run. And every time the one that is in and facing plays and the ball goes out of the field that is four runs and every time the one that is in and facing plays and the ball goes out of the field without touching the ground on the way that is six runs. And every time the ball goes from the one that is in and facing to one of the eleven that are on and is caught by that one then that is out and every time the ball from the one that is bowling hits the stumps that is out and every time the ball hits the one that is in when it would otherwise have hit the stumps that is out and in each case the one that was in is out. And there are other reasons for the one that was in to be out. Then when all who have gone in are out the runs are added up and then the eleven that were on go off and the other eleven come on and two of the first eleven go in and it begins again only the elevens have changed round. It begins again the same thing happens only with the elevens changed round. The eleven that have been in are now all on and the eleven that were on go in one by one after the first two. It's the same as it was before only the other way round. Sometimes this happens twice the eleven go in twice and the other eleven go on twice and sometimes it happens only once. And as before when all those that were in are out the runs are added up and if the runs are more than those of the first eleven that were in then these eleven have won but if the runs add up to less than that then the first eleven have won. That is then the result. That is what is called a result. That is the result of all this that has happened. But if it rains before this is finished there is no result.

TONY LOPEZ

from Radial Symmetry

A smooth laminar stream dissolved the surface.
Mist drifted over the pool of London. I woke
In the abstract sea of unspecified emotion.
Big tour operators are working to patch this
Through a headset. An uncle running up to bowl,
Someone sampling smut. Taste of lemons and oysters.
Music has downsized in tune with the casual look
Now transcending fashion as such. Radiation
And sudden exposure to market forces
Stripped out early consumer activity.
Should another mail arrive from Europe today
Be sure to be clear that we have completely
Conflicting visions of the future. Tick if you
Would prefer not to receive this material.

NICK WHITTOCK

Fiery James Fallkners

FIERY	JAMES	FALLKNERS		
m faces slack		just pie well	brainsre half	up 4 trends
m kidneys				
free trade		burn in (the)		put down left
wing tirades		small of m backll	ver follow	trends
		never learn	wellm not go	ing
2 slow life		cause ev	ery steps	a dragn pieces
of kite materi		als ya ne	ver catch come	up 4 a snatch from
from thegre		just ev	er brainsre half	snatch from hell once
store man		causals think think	well 2 fast 2	while m
jack burning		just think think	well 2 fast 2	write

ring think think

2 fast

burn burn

2 work burn

sat drank while dreams

	ing	while m	put down write	while m	put. burn work burn work	(3w)
follow		while m	end all ing	write	end. ing while m	(6w)
brainsre half	ing	while m	end all don	trends	put. write write	(2w)
y steps		while m	burn work down sat	trends	burn work. sat while m	
think think	left	while m	down write	trends	sat. left burn work	
caster the	snatch	while m	burn work burn	while m	snatch. trends end	(1wb)

eat this gren		als pie well	think think	leftade
musical		al tirades	well think think	while
i said			well trade	end all don
caster the		al tirades	well trade	burn workade
ya ne		small of m backll	ver	up for snatch
not go		als materi	er burning	snatch froming
3 decades		cause slack	er burning	up 4 put
2 fast 2		small of m backll	verman	put burn
y steps		2 fast		put downing
follow		cause theyre	vermateri	write

2 fast

big things

2 write think

4 3 decades

	burn work	while m	down put	write	end. write snatch	(2w)
ring think think	ing	while m	end all sat	trends	end. left left	(2w)
jack burning	ing. sat	while m	put down snatch	trends	put. burn work sat.	
store man		while m	burn work down snatch	write	burn work. snatch while m	(3w)
free trade	ing	while m	snatch from put	trends	end. write write	
of kite materi	end	while m	ingade[redacted]	write	sat. left while m	(3w)

FIERT	JAMES	FALLKNERS		
skeins slip lines		outsourced or	bugeyed	in m rock
bones on		marx shins (raark)		hammie ute
parakeet		the grampampians	or joyces	rock
themselves colours		sucking creeks	or bugeyed	things
weve n event?		out raark	or fiery	puss platy sourced ham
burrow caught or bowled		out objects	or fiery	in m ray
thats for runs		out raark	or continuum	raymie things
exchange		out bugeyed	or continuum	ore ore
sub manta		whale shins		puss
night blooming		whale shins		rock
eye creek dog	how whale bowl			

watto
value

crownie full
goor platy

dodginess	things	ore ore	hammie puss	ore ore	hamstring crownie crownie	(3w)
shoe of joyces	nong	ore ore	eleven things	puss	helmstring things ore ore	(6w)
cricket continuum	things	ore ore	eleven helms	rock	hamstring puss puss	(2w)
jills fiery	nong	ore ore	crowniemie goor	rock	crowniestring goor ore ore	
sprayed bugeyed	ute	ore ore	hoojee puss	rock	goorstring ute crownie	
clararake	ray	ore ore	crownie full	ore ore	raystring rock helmet	(1nb

jessamin		outsourced or	blooming	ute full
of bugs shade		out colours	or blooming	ore ore
cestrum			keet	eleven helmets
clararke		out colours	or keet	crownie full
new objects		the grampampians	or creek dog	in m rays
sprayed bugeyed		out caught or bowled	or manta	eleven rays
splitting creeks		outlines	or manta	in m ham
cricket continuum		the grampampians	or change	ham full
jills fiery		whale shins		hammie things
shoe of joyces		out for runs	or caught or bowled	puss
dodginess		whale shins		rock

watto
value

things full
goor platypus

eye creek dog	crownie	ore ore	noojee ham	puss	helmstring pussray
night blooming	things	ore ore	eleven goor	rock	helmstring ute
sub manta	thingsstringgoor	ore ore	hammie ray	rock	hamstring crowniegoor
exchange	nong	ore ore	crowniemie rays	puss	crowniestring rays ore ore
parakeet	things	ore ore	raymie ham	rock	helmstring puss
borrow caught or bowled	helmet	ore ore	things full	puss	puss

(2n

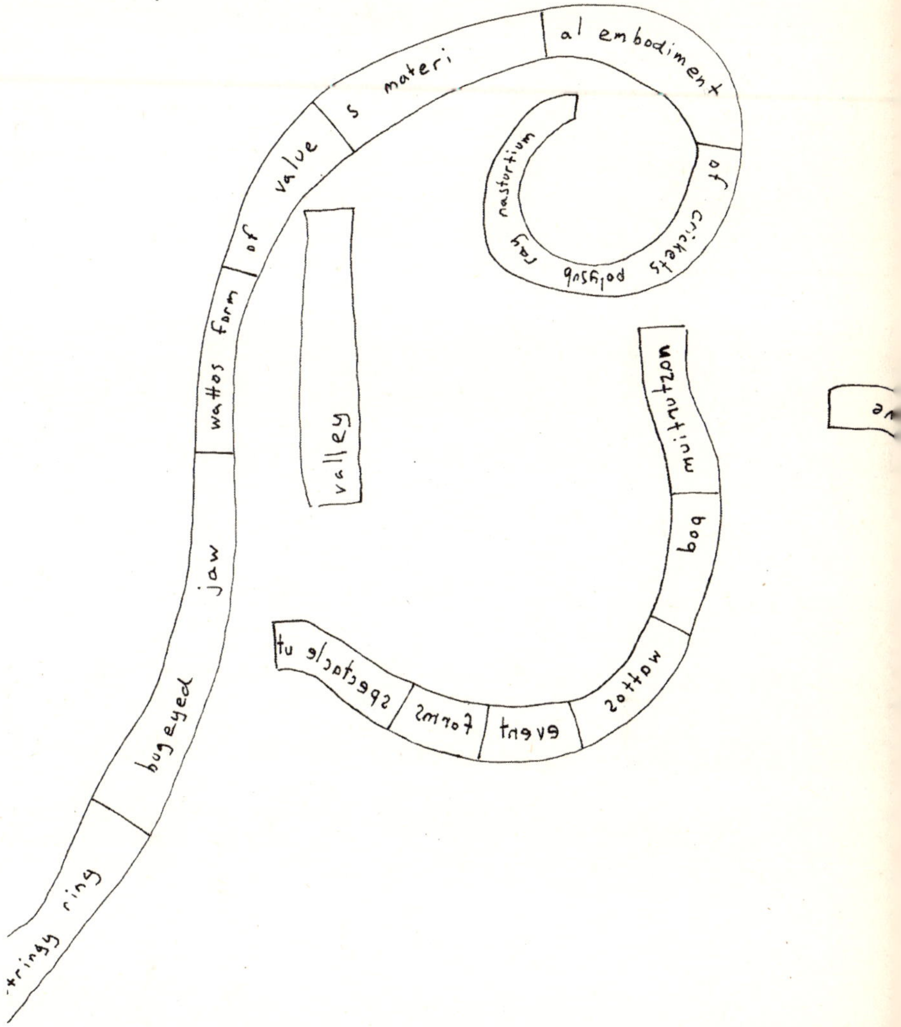
stringy ring
bugeyed
jaw
wattos form
of
value
s materi
al embodiment
of
crickets
polysub
ray
nasturtium
valley
bog
wattos
event
forms
spectacle ut

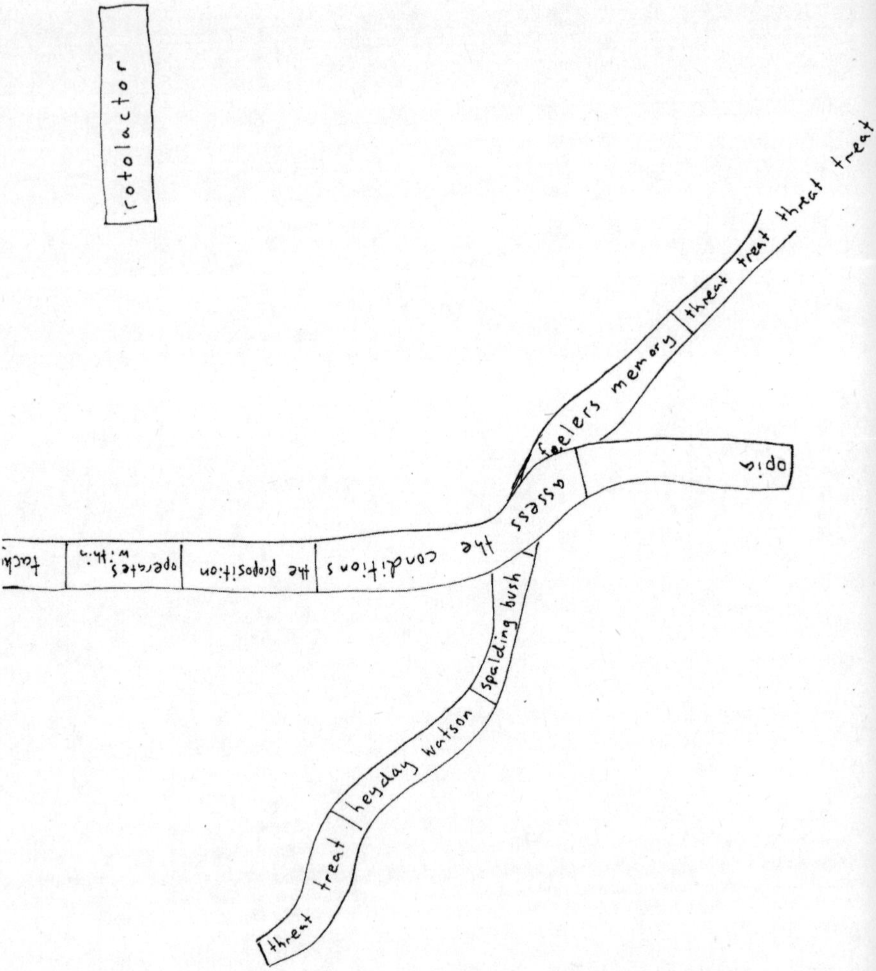
rotolactor
threat treat threat treat
feelers memory
opic
assess
the conditions
the proposition
operates within
tacki
spalding bush
heyday watson
threat treat

FIERY JAMES FALLKNERS

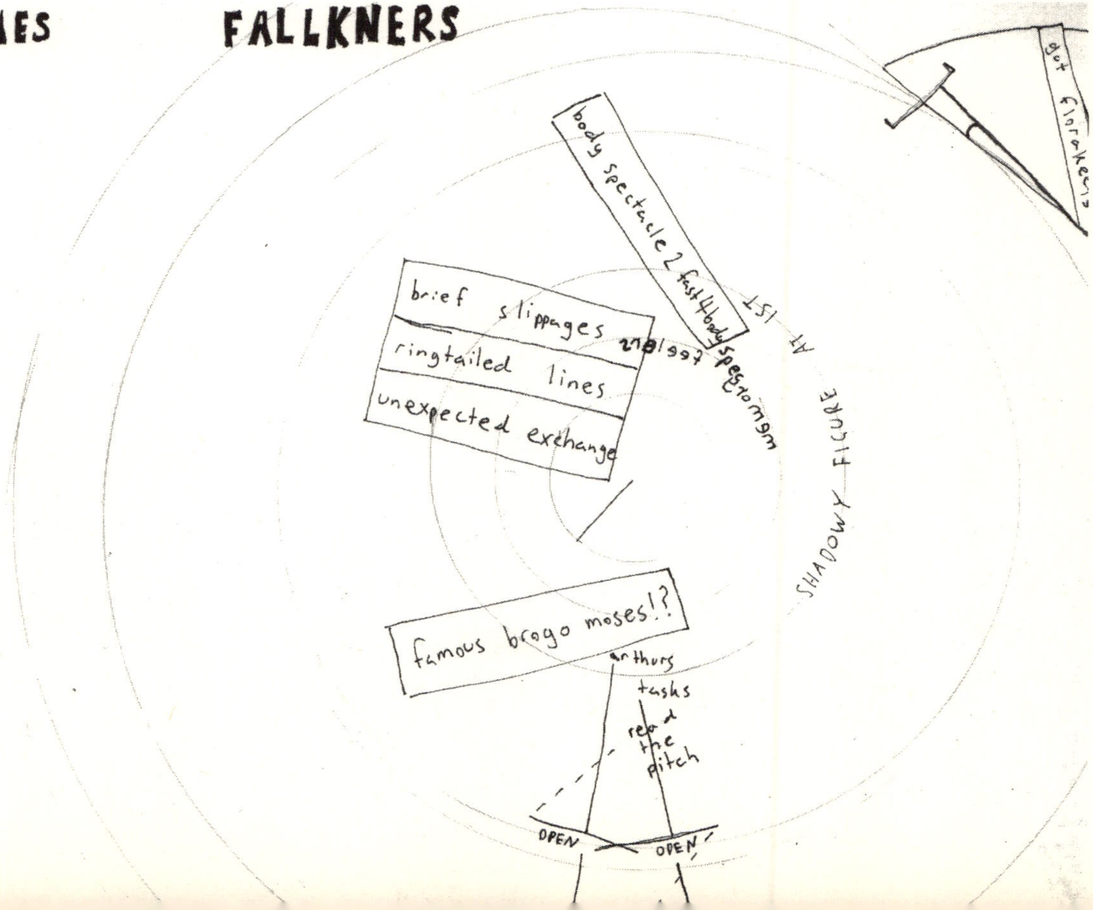

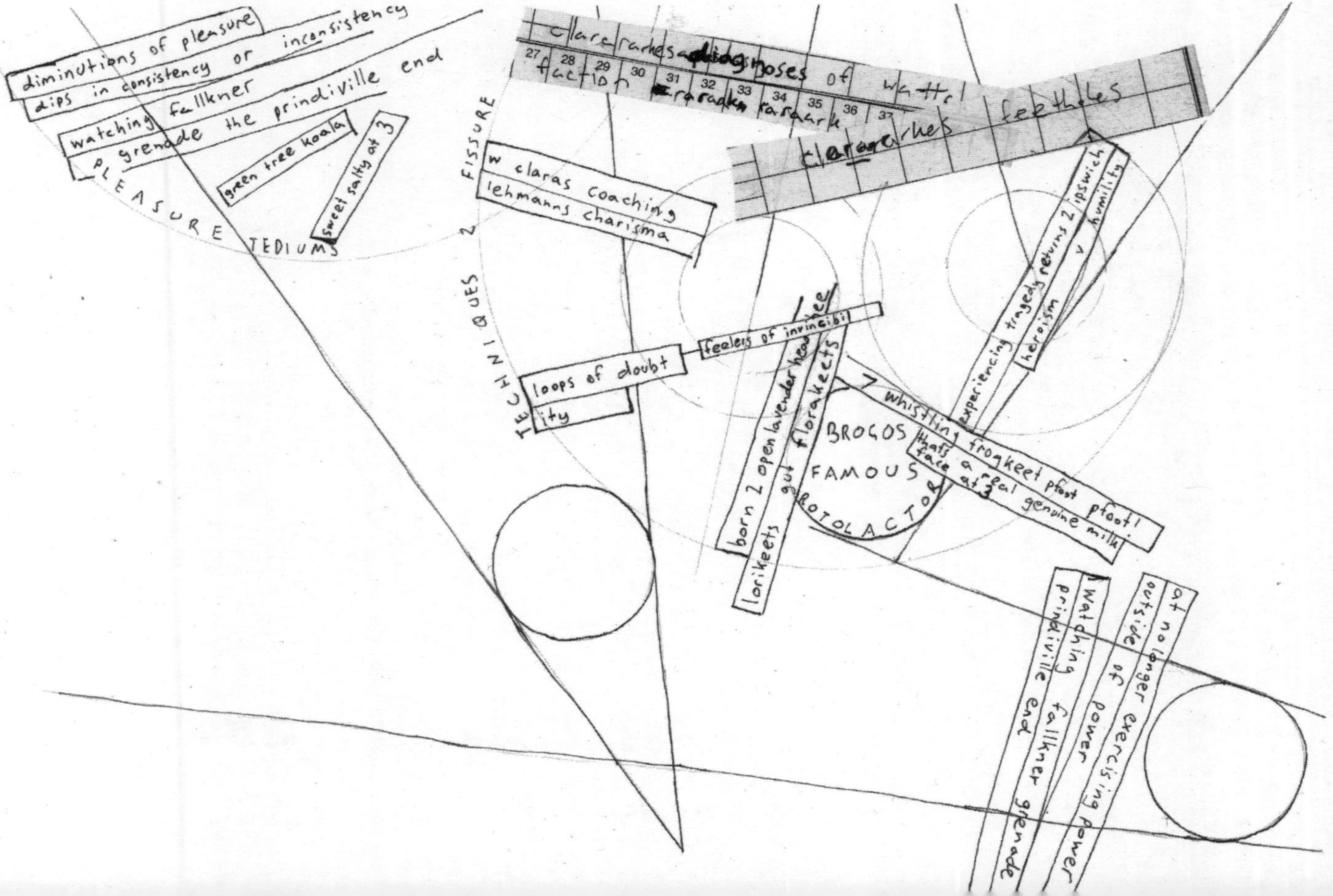

diminutions of pleasure
dips in consistency or inconsistency
watching fallkner
grenade the prindiville end
PLEASURE
PLEASURE TEDIUMS
green tree koala
sweet salty at 3
FISSURE 2 TECHNIQUES
w claras coaching
lehmanns charisma
loops of doubt
ity
feelers of invincibil
born 2 open lavender head
lorikeets
gut florakeets
BROGOS
FAMOUS
ROTOLACTOR
whistling frogkeet pfoot pfoot!
thats a real genuine milk
face at 3
experiencing tragedy returns 2 ipswich
heroism v humility
moses of
fact
feethes
at no longer exercising power
outside of power
watching fallkner grenade
prindiville end

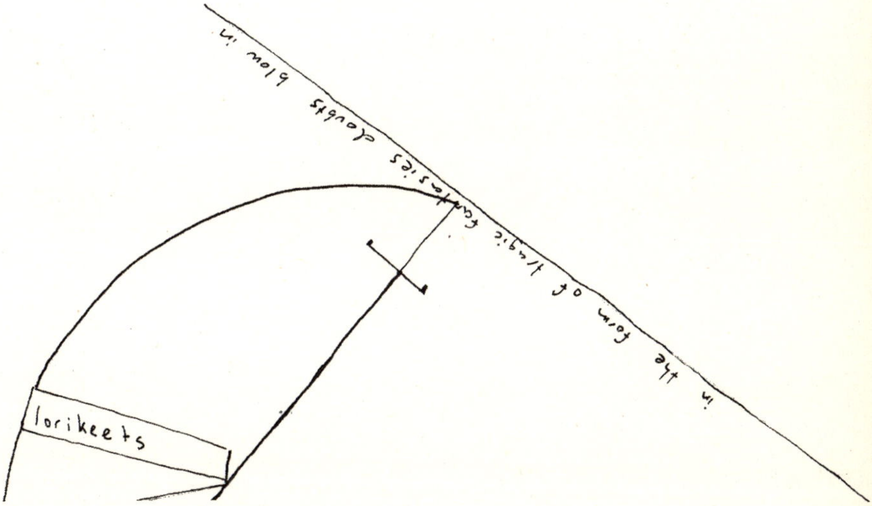
in the form of tragic fantasies clouds blow in
lorikeets

BIOGRAPHIES

TIM ATKINS used to watch cricket at New Road, Worcester, in the days of the John Player League (with free JPS fags handed out to ex-public-school boys in regimental ties at the pavilion end) and the days of the Benson & Hedges Cup (with its free fags tossed out of buckets in the direction of farmers of less refined & indeterminate sexuality at the swampy and windswept end of the ground). His Salt Press volume, *Folklore* (a *Daily Telegraph* book of the year) is an extended hallucinatory sequence which takes place whilst falling into a dream in the ditch by the side of the River Severn during a JPS Sunday league match between Worcestershire and Surrey in the summer of 1975. 'Petrarch 23' was published in *Atkins Collected Petrarch*, © 2014 by Tim Atkins.

OLIVER BAGGOTT is a totally pissy artist, alives and working in london, eng...being a little bit aussie qualifies in the cricket stakes...

NIA DAVIES likes to stroke the surface of cricket. Her publications are *Then spree* (2012, Salt) and *Çekoslovakyalılastıramadıklarımızdanmısınız or Long Words* (forthcoming 2016, Hafan/Boiled String). She edits *Poetry Wales* and works on international literature projects.

KEN EDWARDS' books include the poetry collections *Good Science* (1992), *eight + six* (2003), *No Public Language: Selected Poems 1975-95* (2006), *Bird Migration in the 21st Century* (2006), *Songbook* (2009), the novels *Futures* (1998) and *Country Life* (2015) and the prose works *Bardo* (2011) and *Down With Beauty* (2013). He has been editor/publisher of the small press Reality Street since 1993. He lives in Hastings, on the south coast of England, where he plays bass guitar and sings with The Moors, a band he co-founded with Elaine Edwards. He never got the hang of playing the game of cricket and has remained an avid spectator on television, resenting every penny paid to Mr. Murdoch for the privilege.

GREGORIO FONTAINE. Singing poet from Chile. Currently lives in London. Combining field recording, huayno rhythms, and sound poetry, his work has been described as one of ramshackle and unique songs, whose effect is hallucinatory, corrosive; both strange and beautiful. He has been an active exponent of experimental poetry in Chile; with works published in Chile, Mexico and the UK. His only knowledge of cricket is that of occasionally seeing people playing it in parks and that his brother played it for a while. www.gregoriofonten.com

CHRIS HALL was born in 1945, grew up in Chatham, north Kent, and has lived in South Wales for over thirty years. He has been writing and reading his poems since the mid-'60s, operating, over the past couple of decades, on both sides of the Wales/England border. His most recent publications include his collection of 'weird tales' *Balladz f Bedlam* and a reissue of his long poem *Bneath Cragshhaddo* based on his experiences while living in Prague soon after the 'Velvet Revolution', which first appeared in 2000 but has now undergone a substantial revision. His work has also appeared in *Scintilla* and *Tears in the Fence,* and he is a regular contributor to the Hay-on-Wye magazine *Quirk*. He has also released a CD *No Ifs.* An exhibiting artist as well as a poet, he has a studio in the Apple Store Gallery, Hereford and over recent years has had one-person shows at St David's Cathedral; the Barker Gallery, Pontypool; The Artworkhouse, Abergavenny; and the Kickplate Gallery, Abertillery. He is currently based in Abergavenny, Monmouthshire. He writes: 'I am very much a non-sporty person, and this is the only poem I have written on the subject, and likely so to remain. It stems from my boyhood days, and has its seeds in my dislike of the games days at my grammar school where I was compelled to both play rugby union football, and abandon the soccer version which I had previously enjoyed as a junior schoolboy. As far as rugby itself was concerned, I learnt quite quickly that it was possible to loiter at the opposite end of the field where the more muscle-bound participants were too busily engrossed in inflicting various degrees of ill-health on each other's frames to pay much heed to me or to threaten any serious harm to my person. Cricket, however, was another matter, as one was utterly exposed in the most alarming way to not only physical injury from the lethal ball, but also to a considerable degree of taunting, ridicule and downright unpopularity as a result of cowardice at the crease or ineptitude in the field. Hence my antipathy to the game, owing to the deep and permanent disturbance as a result the traumatic experiences inflicted upon my psyche at an impressionable and vulnerable stage of my adolescence.'

JOHN HALL is a poet, teacher and essayist, with recent books from etruscan, Shearsman and Reality Street, who became obsessively interested in cricket as a child in Africa in the 1950s and never fully recovered; his playing days, which became increasingly frivolous, are long over. TMS, Cricinfo and Channel 5 highlights keep him engaged and informed.

ALAN HALSEY's recent books are *Rampant Inertia* (Shearsman) and *Versions of Martial* (Knives Forks & Spoons). In 1973 he scored a career-defining half-century batting for the National Library for the Blind against the Royal National Institute for the Blind (one sighted player allowed per team). He spends his retirement listening to TMS.

BEN HICKMAN is Lecturer in Modern Poetry at the University of Kent. His books include *Crisis and the US Avant-Garde: Poetry and Real Politics* (Edinburgh University Press, 2015) and *Later Britain* (Oystercatcher Press, 2014). In his playing days for Hedge End CC in Hampshire, it was rumoured Hickman had the most elegant leave outside of Marylebone.

JEFF HILSON's publications include *stretchers* (2006, Reality Street), *Bird bird* (2009, Landfill) and *In The Assarts* (2010, Veer Books). From 1974-1982 he played in various school 1st & 2nd XIs. He also edited *The Reality Street Book of Sonnets* (2008, Reality Street). Improbably his highest score of 64 not out was achieved without spectacles. Poems have also appeared in magazines including *Onedit*, *Jacket 2*, *Open Letter*, *English* and *Fence*. Unaccountably in 1983 he was dropped from the school 3rd XI before taking up the game again at Cambridge University. Recent work has been published by award winning presses such as Crater and Oystercatcher. Between 1993 and 2007 he opened the bowling for South London Cricket legends Energy Exiles for whom on a very green wicket he once achieved 7 for 24. He teaches Creative Writing at the University of Roehampton and runs the reading series Xing the Line. He retired from cricket, unhurt, in 2008.

PETER HUGHES, night watchman of choice for his school 20-20 team, is a poet and qualified cricket coach. As a player he specialised in ill-judged lofted drives to long on, and bowling picturesque long hops. He was quite a good fielder. His greatest cricketing achievement was in flooring a sadistic woodwork teacher with a largely accidental beamer during a lunchtime net. His subsequent attempt to create a commemorative plaque for the school hall using only a soldering iron and an unhinged desktop was insensitively suppressed by fascistic school management agents. '*Quite Frankly* 64' and '*Quite Frankly* 231' from *Quite Frankly: After Petrarch's Sonnets* (Reality Street, 2015) reproduced with the kind permission of Ken Edwards at Reality Street.

PETER JAEGER is a Canadian poet now living in the UK. He is the author of several books and is Professor of Poetics at Roehampton University in London. He once saw some people playing cricket in a park in Canada's wealthiest city, Mississauga.

ANTONY JOHN's *now than it used to be, but in the past* is published by Veer. His poems have appeared in numerous magazines and anthologies. When he was a boy, his father played cricket for Kempston.

SARAH KELLY is a poet, text based artist and hand paper maker. At 14 she had a playground crush on a boy in her class who was shy, quiet and kind. He played in the cricket team and she would go and watch. They smiled at each other but never really spoke. One day he delivered fifty roses to her door. A few weeks later he was convicted for arson, bomb related possession and corporate fraud.

TONY LOPEZ's most recent poetry book is *Only More So* (Shearsman, 2012); a new edition of *False Memory* was published at the same time. He has always liked the song 'That'll Be the Day' by Buddy Holly and The Crickets. 'Radial Symmetry' from *False Memory*, © 2003 by Tony Lopez.

CHIAKI MATSUBAYASHI is a Digital Cinema Subtitler and translator who lives in London. She is not a fan of cricket.

松林千秋はロンドン在住の翻訳家。現職はデジタルシネマ用の字幕データ製作。クリケットのファンではない。

MICHAELA MEISE is an artist from Berlin, Germany. Her main media are sculpture in wood and ceramic, as well as watercolours and artists' books. The only time she witnessed a cricket match was in a park in Dartford, where she had a school visit at 16. She remembers the calm atmosphere of the game.

GERALDINE MONK was born in Blackburn, Lancashire. First published in the 1970s, her poetry has appeared extensively in the UK and America. She is an affiliated poet to the Centre of Poetry and Poetics at the University of Sheffield. She writes: 'At the age of 14 my family moved to a house which overlooked the Church & Oswaldtwistle Cricket Club, and from that day cricket literally became a backdrop in my life. My father was briefly the steward of the social club until his untimely death in 1984.'

MONTENEGRO FISHER are a collective art and poetry project of Luna Montenegro and Adrian Fisher. They investigate text and performance through ritual and the body. They show their work in art galleries, cinemas and public spaces.

They are in possession of a miniature Warwickshire cricket bat signed by the team in 1978 and sponsored by a formerly large building and construction company. Both Montenegro and Fisher are left-handed batsmen. mmmmm.org.uk

RICHARD PARKER is an Assistant Professor of American Literature at Dokuz Eylül University in Izmir in Turkey. He has published two full-length collections of poetry and some pamphlets, is the printer of the Crater Press pamphlet series and is working on a monograph about American avant-garde poetics and baseball. He performed intermittently for the non-squad at Felsted Prep. in the early 1990s.

JÈSSICA PUJOL DURAN lives in Izmir, London and Mataró. She was Poet in Residence at the University of Surrey in 2013/14. She writes in Catalan, English and Spanish, and has published her poetry and translations in international magazines and with publishers such as *Tripwire*, *Sibila*, *Hi Zero*, *onedit*, *Alba Londres*, Infinite Editions, *Department*, Crater and *Summerstock*, and in various anthologies. She has a book and a chapbook in English: *Now Worry* (Department, 2012) and *Every Bit of Light* (Oystercatcher Press, 2012). She is the editor of *Alba Londres* (www.albalondres.com), a magazine that publishes Latin American, Iberian and British literature on translation. She is currently finishing a PhD on experimental literature at University College London. She writes: 'Cricket is a foreign sport to a Catalan. When I moved to Kennington (Oval) I began to wonder "why in white and why, here and now, is it raining… all day, really?"'

ANDREW SPRAGG was born in London and lives there. Recent books include *OBJECTS* (Red Ceiling Press, 2014), *A Treatise on Disaster* (Contraband Books, 2013) *To Blart & Kid* (Like This Press, 2013) and *Tether//Replica* (Susakpress/Spiralbound 2015). He also writes music reviews for the Quietus and Bonafide magazine. He lives a stone's throw from the original cow corner at Dulwich College.

EDWARD SUCKLING is an animator based in Norwich, and occasionally bowls leg spin for local side The Kingfishers on a Thursday evening. He studied animation at the Royal College of Art, and his influences include JJ Villard and Shane Warne. You can see examples of his animation work at www.edsuckling.com.

SCOTT THURSTON's most recent book is *Figure Detached, Figure Impermanent* (Oystercatcher, 2014). He co-runs The Other Room poetry series, co-edits the Journal of British and Irish Innovative Poetry, and lectures at the University of Salford. His poems included here emerged out of a few years of committed armchair cricket watching in the late nineties/early noughties when he should have been writing his PhD. 'Red Snowflake', 'Incident Room', 'An Injury Helps', 'I Heard

An Accident, 'Let's Talk About Us', 'Alternate, Slowly' from *Hold: Poems 1994-2004* (Shearsman, 2006) reproduced with the kind permission of Tony Frazer at Shearsman Books.

RHYS TRIMBLE is a poet who vaguely understands the rules of cricket and has a very small beard. www.trimbling.com

LAURA FOSTER TWIGG travelled the world for years and ended up in the land of cricket by dint of marriage. She now lives and works in South London.

CAROL WATTS's most recent poetry collections are *Occasionals* (Reality Street) and *Sundog* (Veer Books). She grew up in a family where cricket had made things possible. Her birth was reported in the sports pages of the Northampton *Chronicle & Echo*. Her father Jim Watts played professionally for Northants from 1959 to 1980, and was a successful captain of the side.

Melbourne poet NICK WHITTOCK's first book *covers* was published by COD in 2004. In 2012 Vagabond published *the doon* as part of their Rare Objects Series. In 2014 *HOWS ITS* was published by Inken Publisch. Nick played his last game of competitive cricket in January 2012. Fielding at mid off for socialist cricket team The Reds he dropped a catch which would have won the game. In the process he shattered his left thumb. The Reds went on to lose the match.

JOSEPHINE WOOD, artist, lives/works London, UK. She writes: 'I like cricket especially the leg guards.'